I0480408

HOW TO DRAW FLOWERS FOR KIDS

Step by Step Guide to Drawing Cute Flowers

By

Serena Davis

AUTHOR BIO

Serena Davis is an artist who lives and works in Los Angeles. From a young age she found that she had a particular talent for drawing, and she spent almost every waking hour as a child, honing her skills by sketching animals, the sea, buildings, and anything else that she found interesting.

Following her attendance at UCLA, Serena did a lot of travelling and visited Australia, southeast Asia, India, and parts of Europe. There she immersed herself in the cultures she found, drawing every day, and living a simple life. When she returned to the USA it was with a huge collection of drawings which she then started to improve upon and sell.

This modest income allowed her to concentrate full time on drawing and before long she had the idea of creating a series of books for children and adults, in which Serena could use her full range of talents to help others develop theirs.

In her spare time, Serena loves to go to the beach on a warm sunny day and sketch the people and animals she sees there. She is constantly developing ideas for new books and enjoys the freedom of being outdoors.

She lives in a small apartment with a tiny garden, but despite this she still manages to grow lots of vegetables which she loves turning into a delicious meal.

A Aster

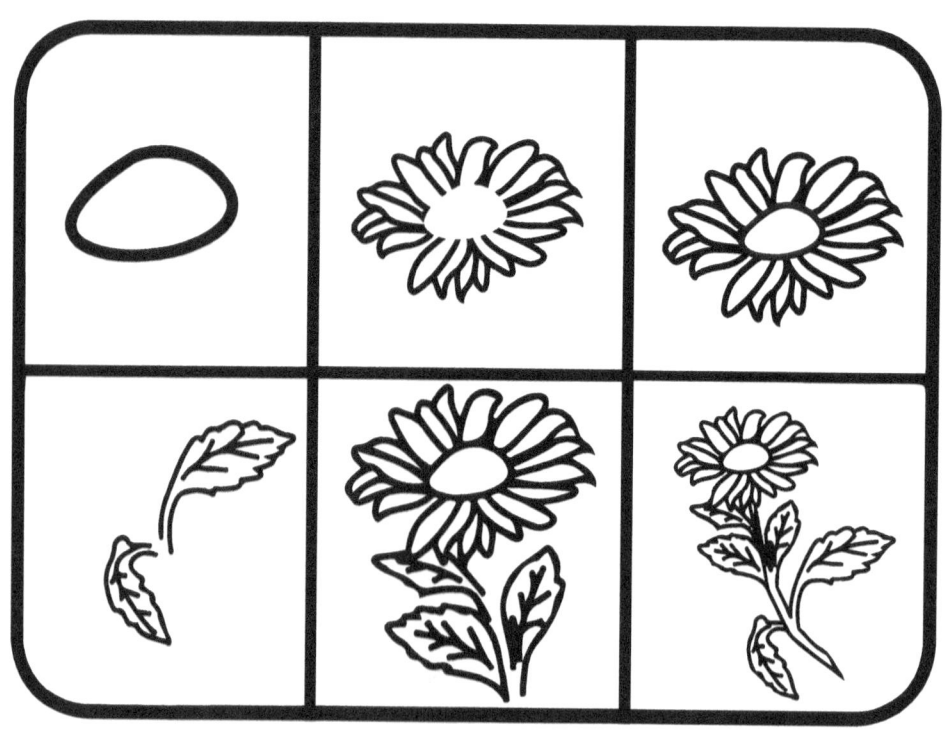

A Anastasia

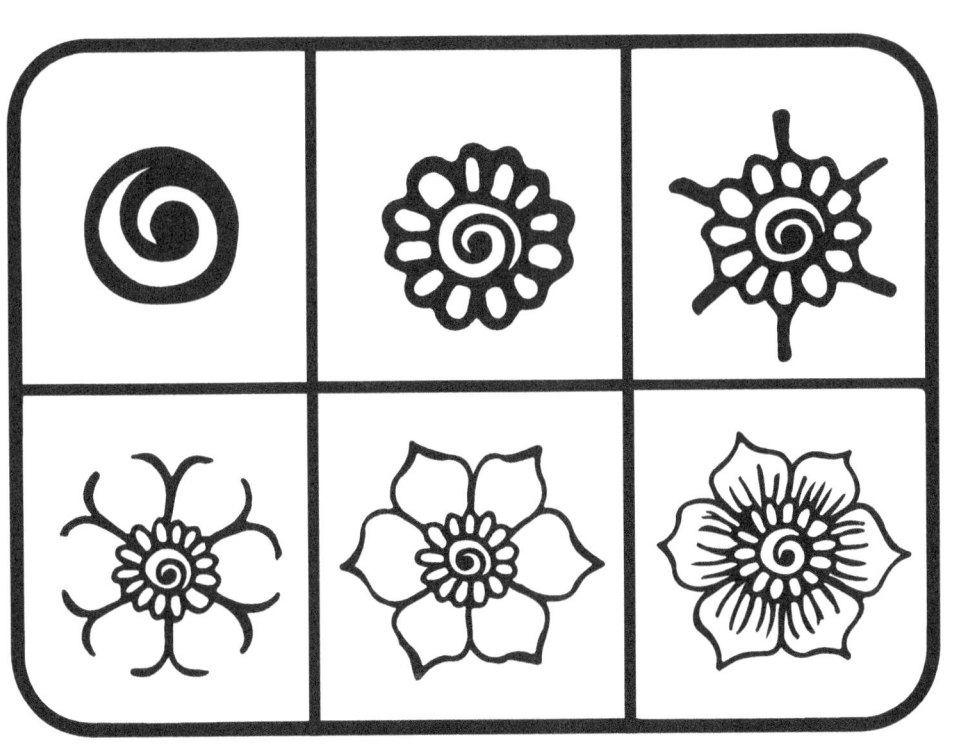

A Acacia

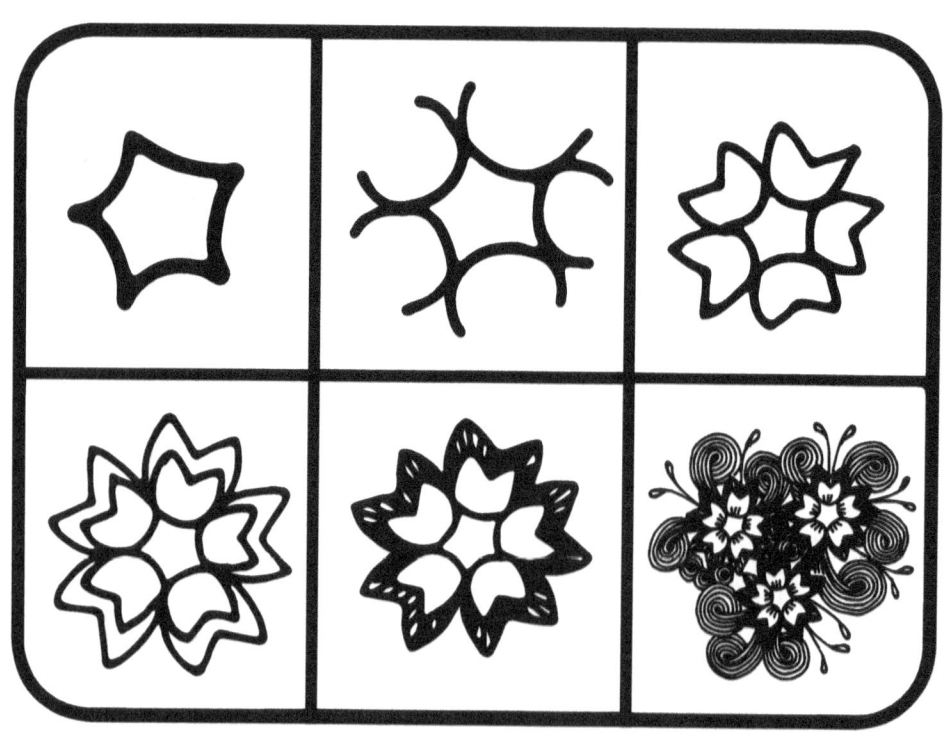

A Anooka

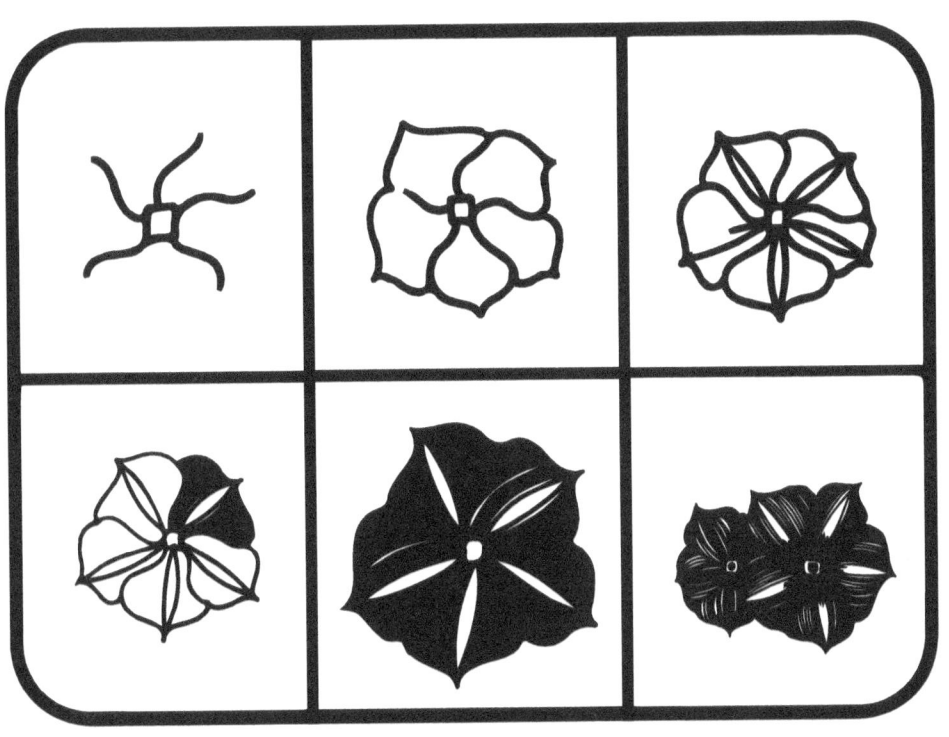

A Atomica

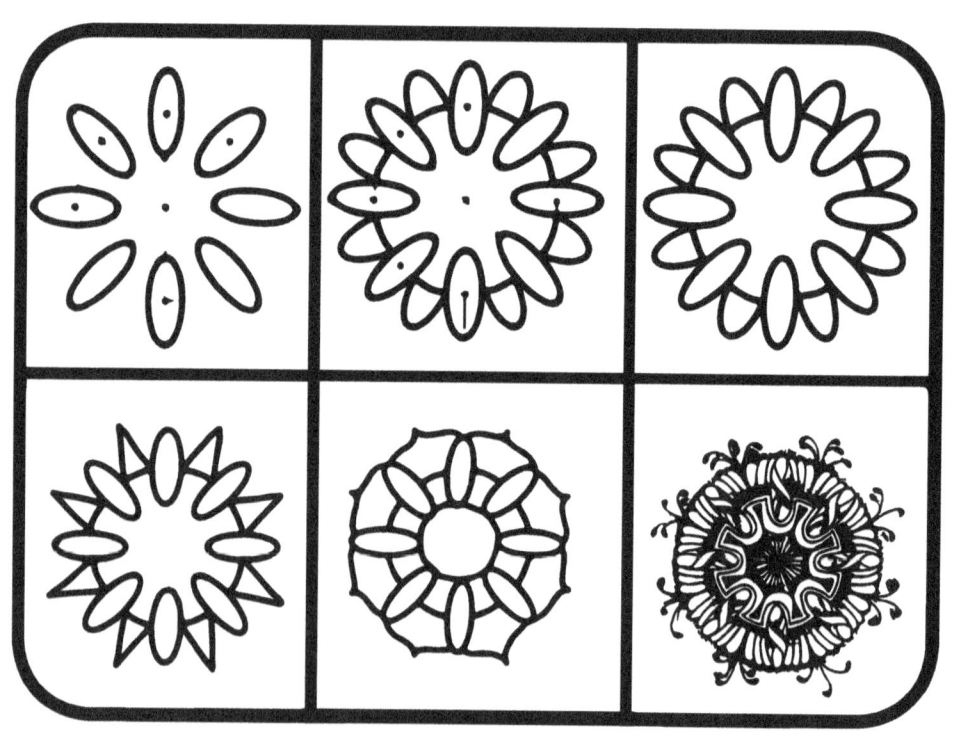

A Azlea

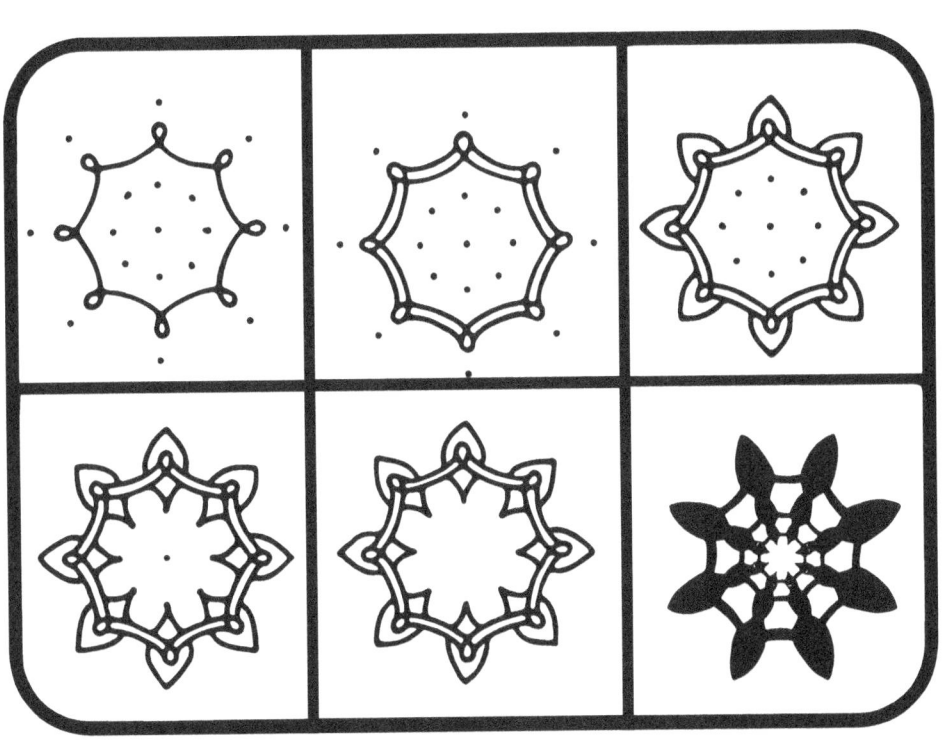

B Barberry

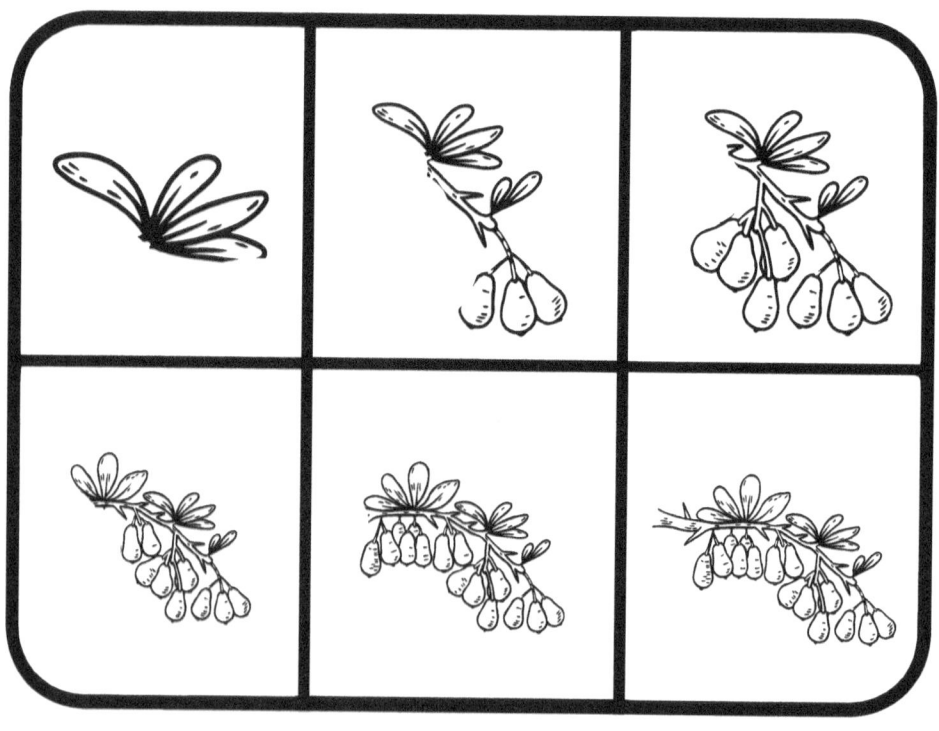

B Balldox

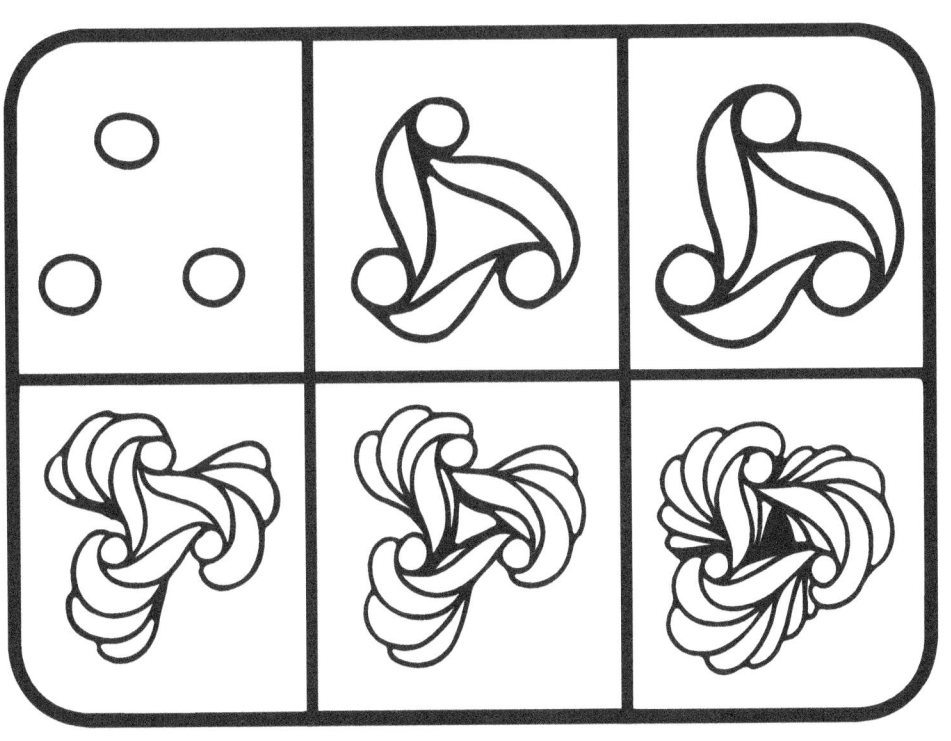

B Barbet

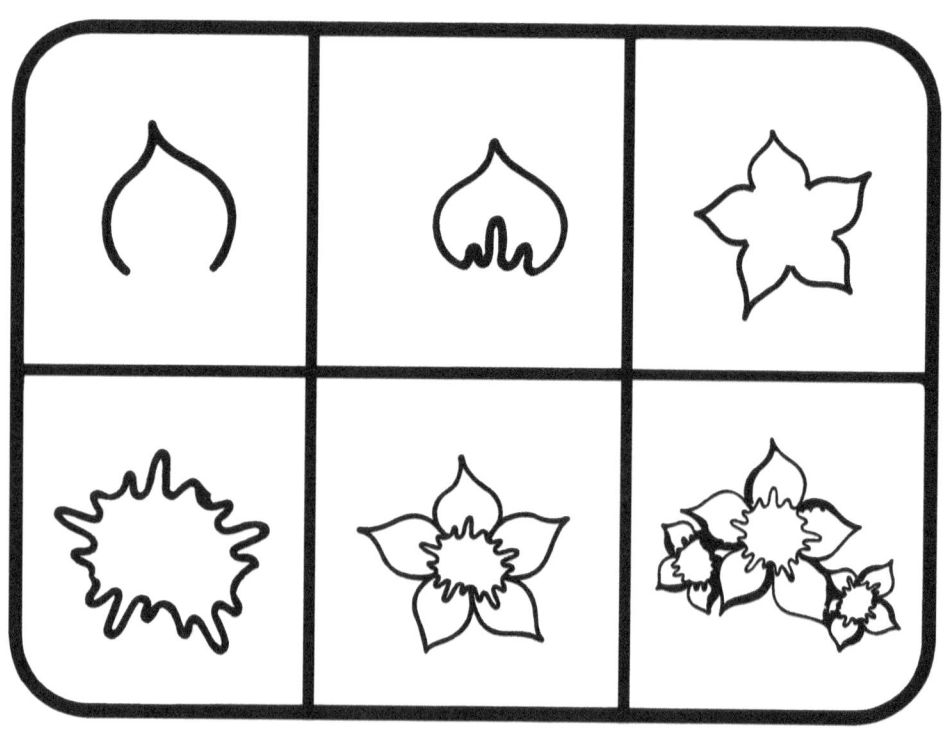

B Barullo

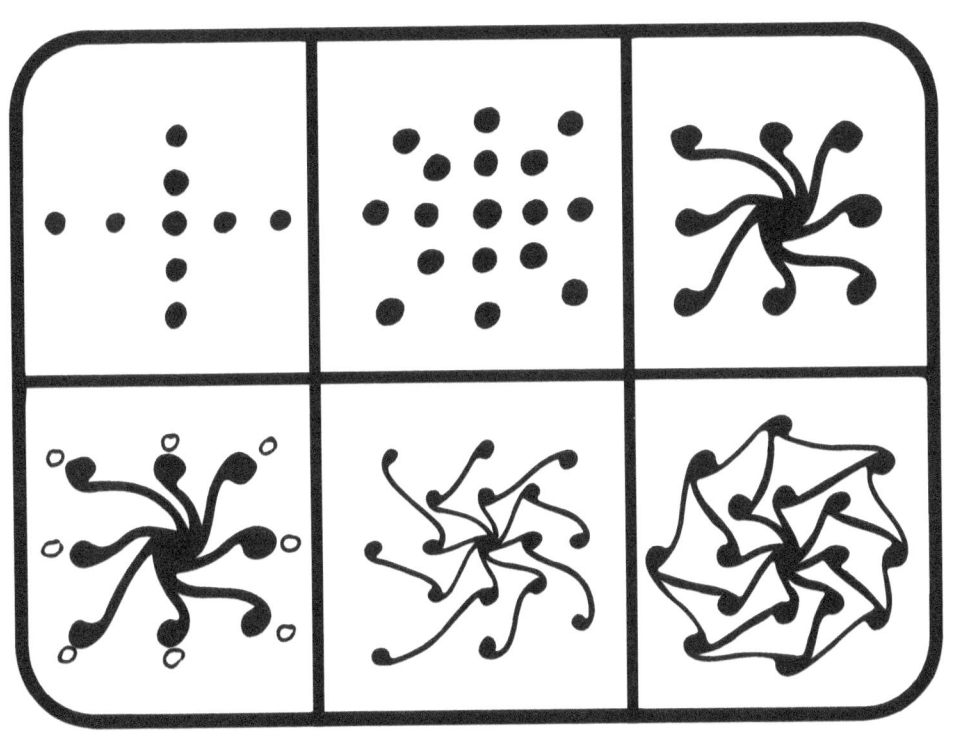

B Cactus

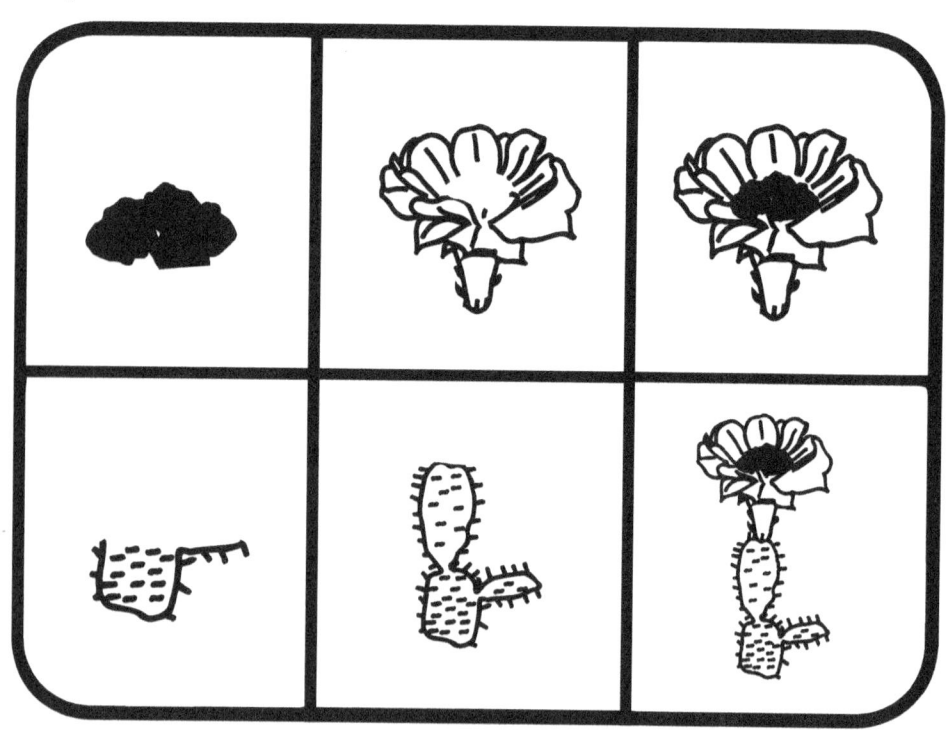

C Chrysanthemum

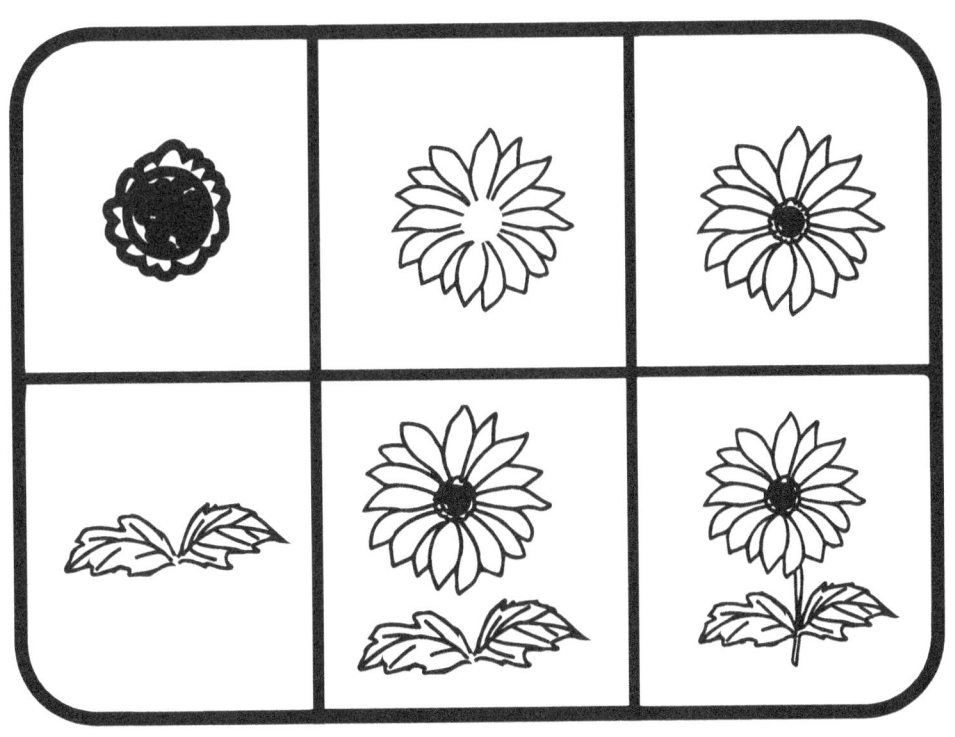

C Columbine

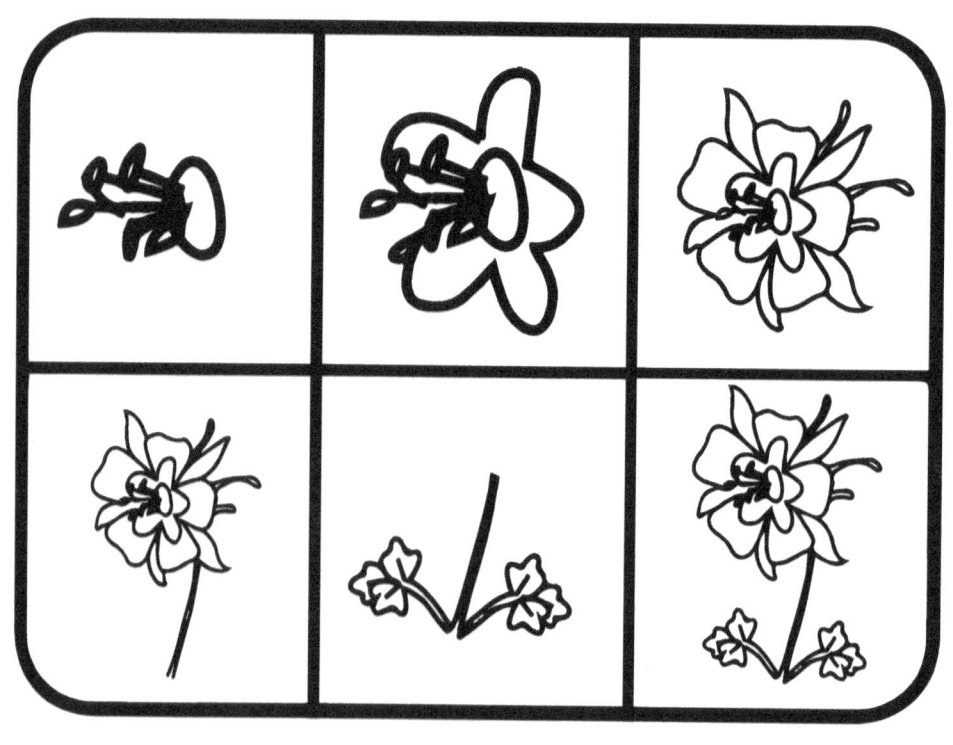

C Carnation

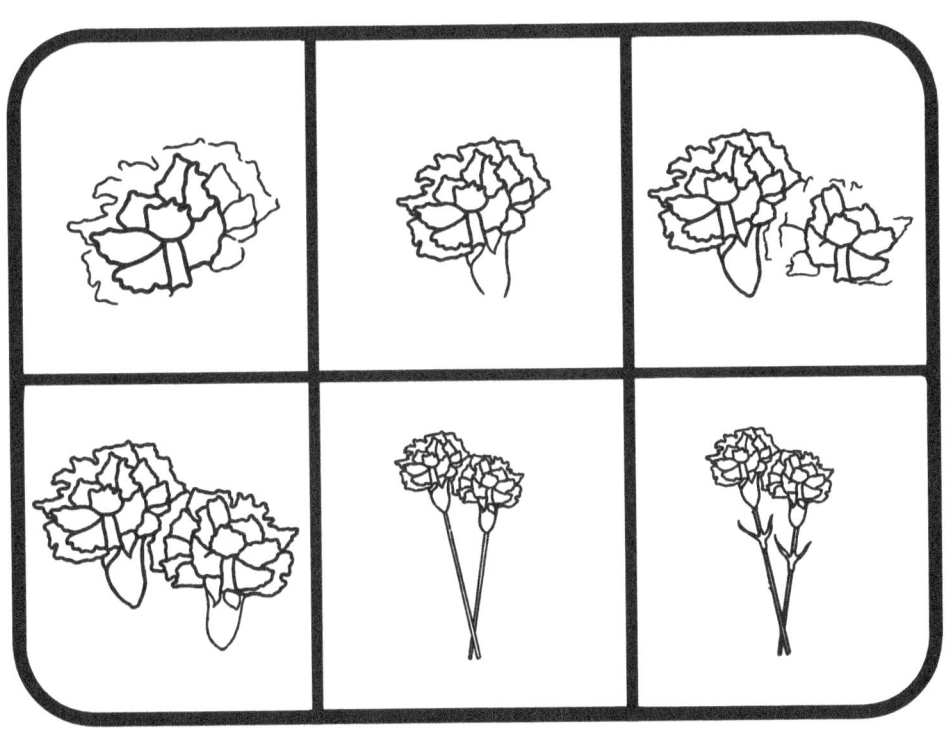

C Calantha

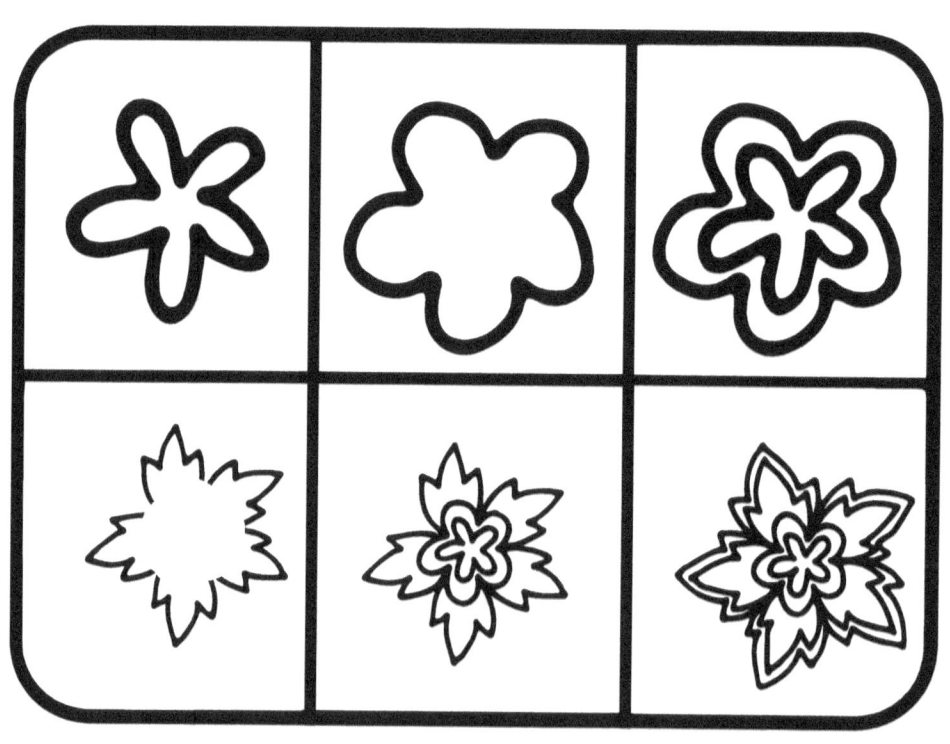

C
Candle Light

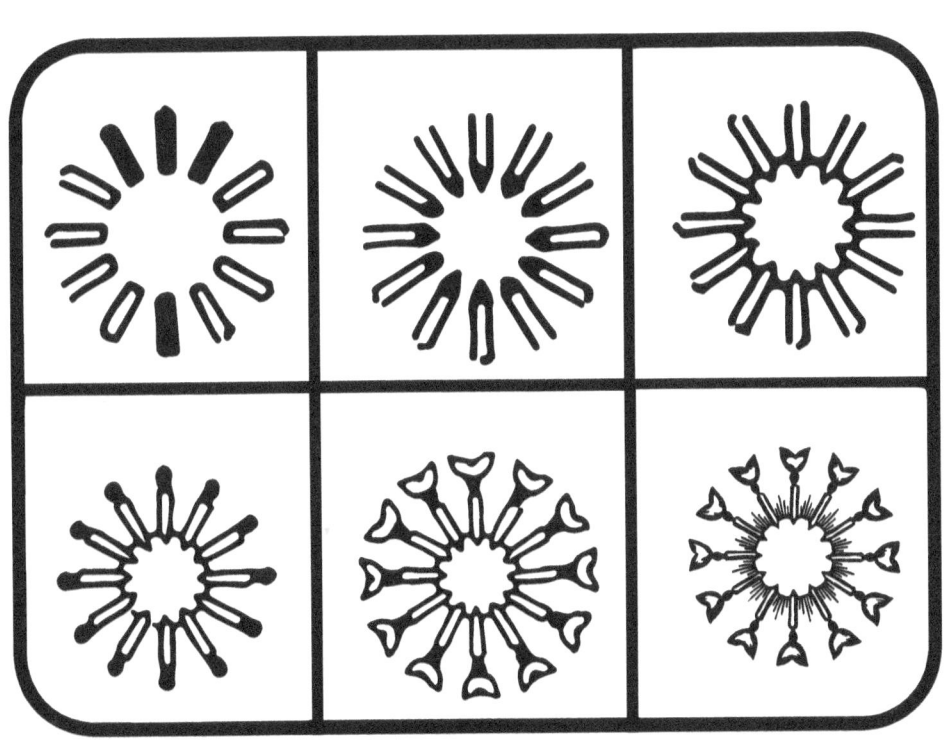

C Chainey

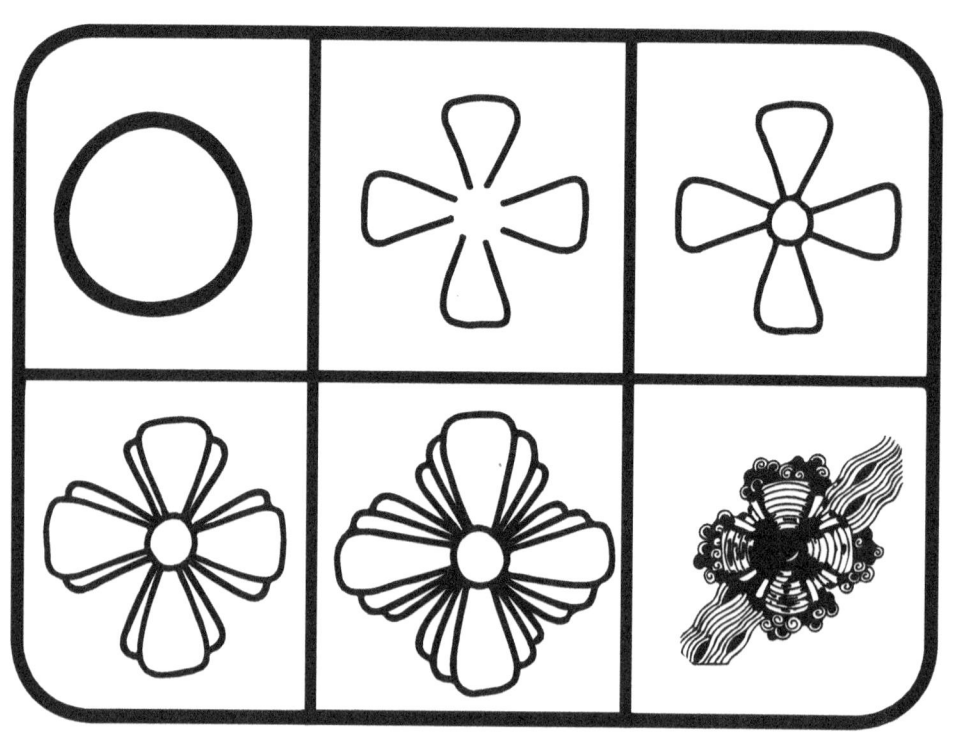

D Daffodil

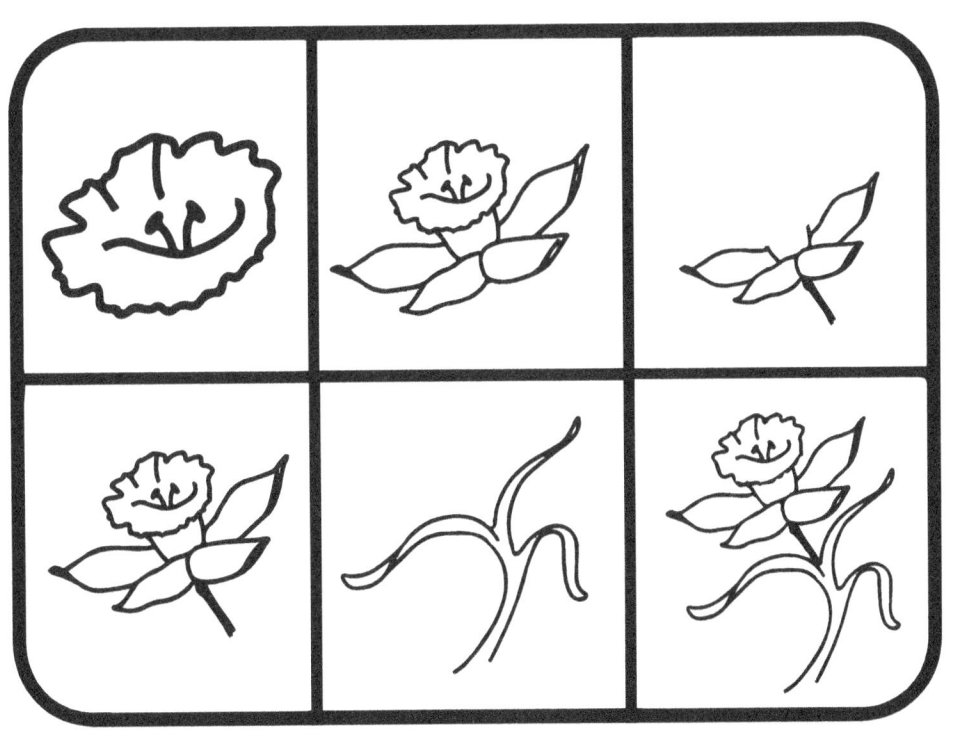

D

Dahlia

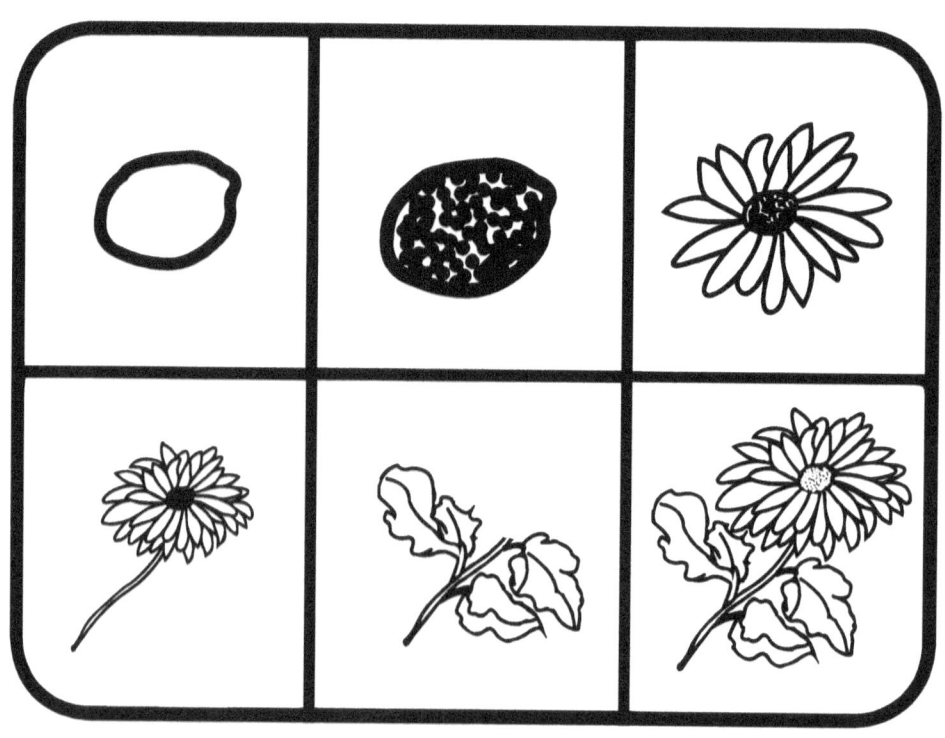

D Daisy

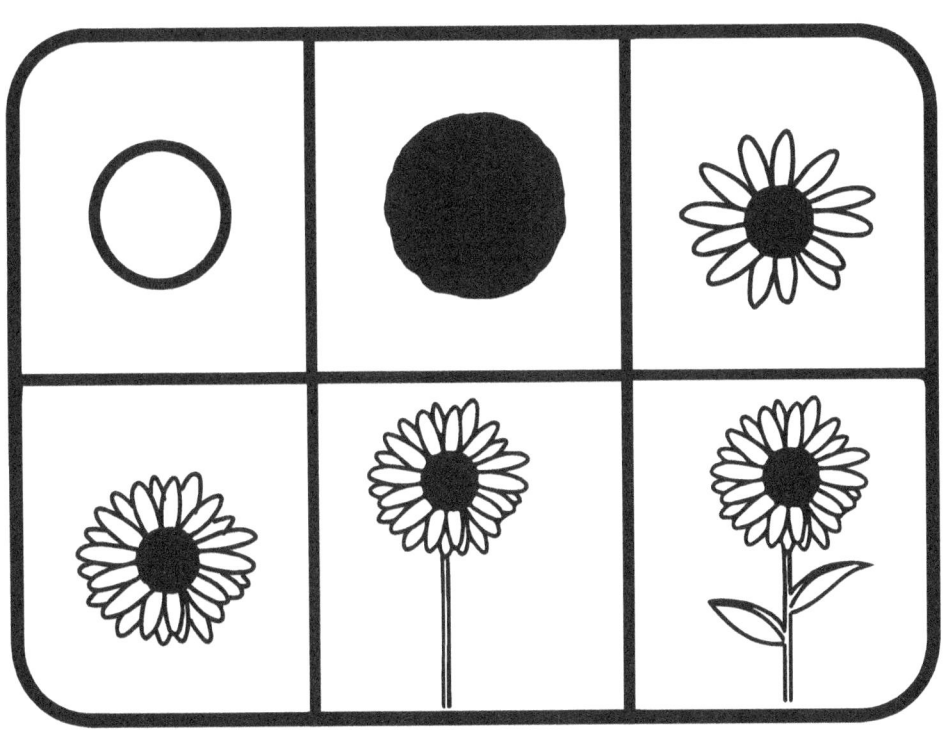

D Dandelion

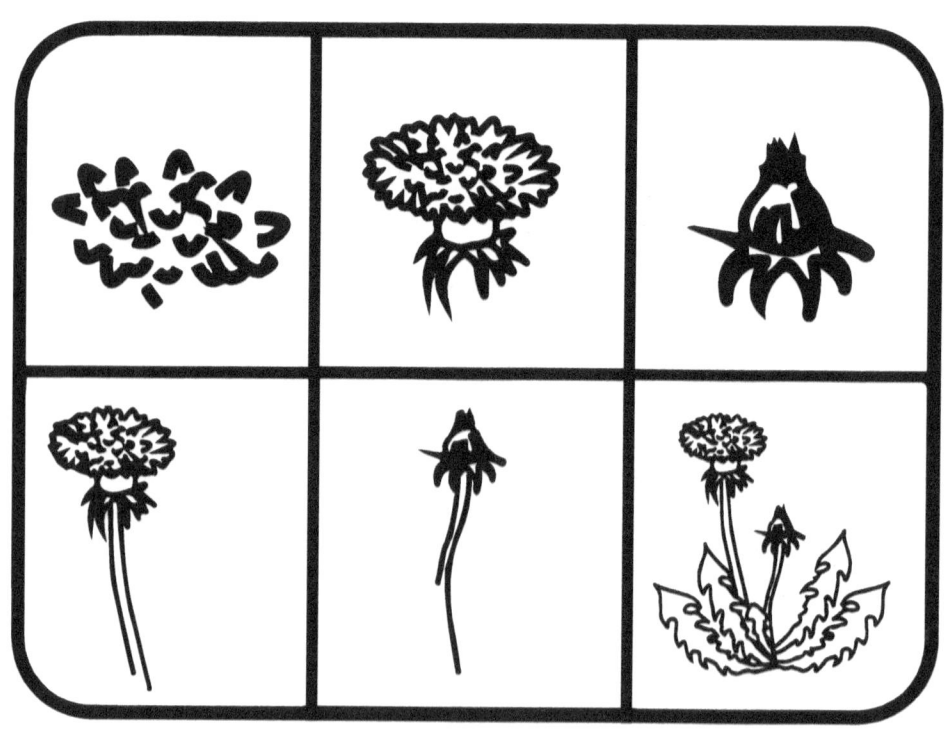

D

Dr Odd

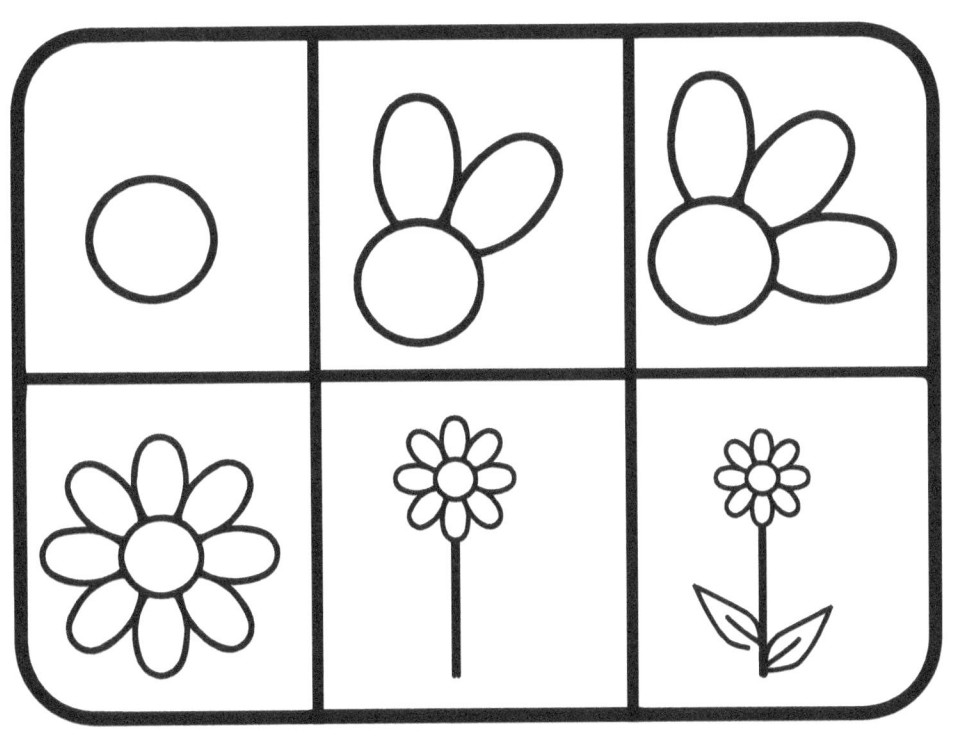

D Dogwood

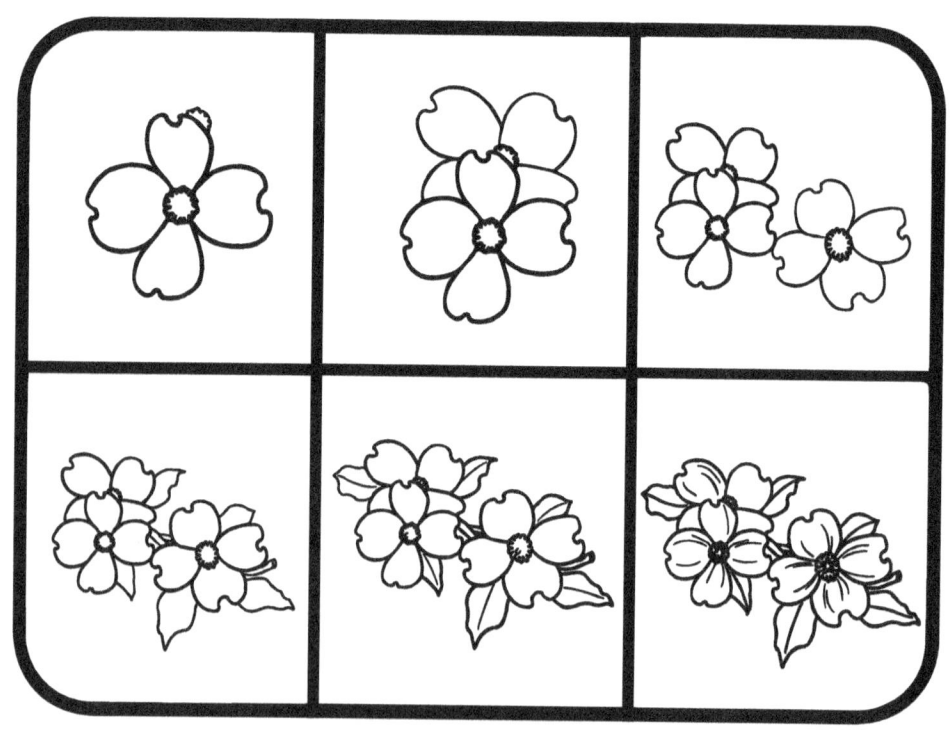

D Dogwood

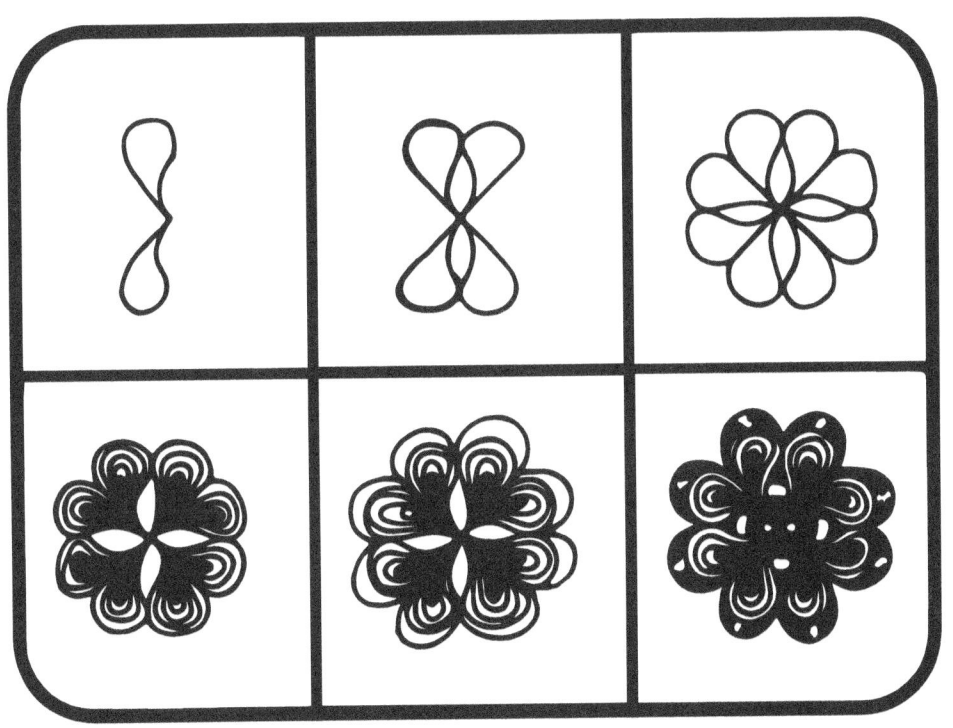

D

Dahlidrops

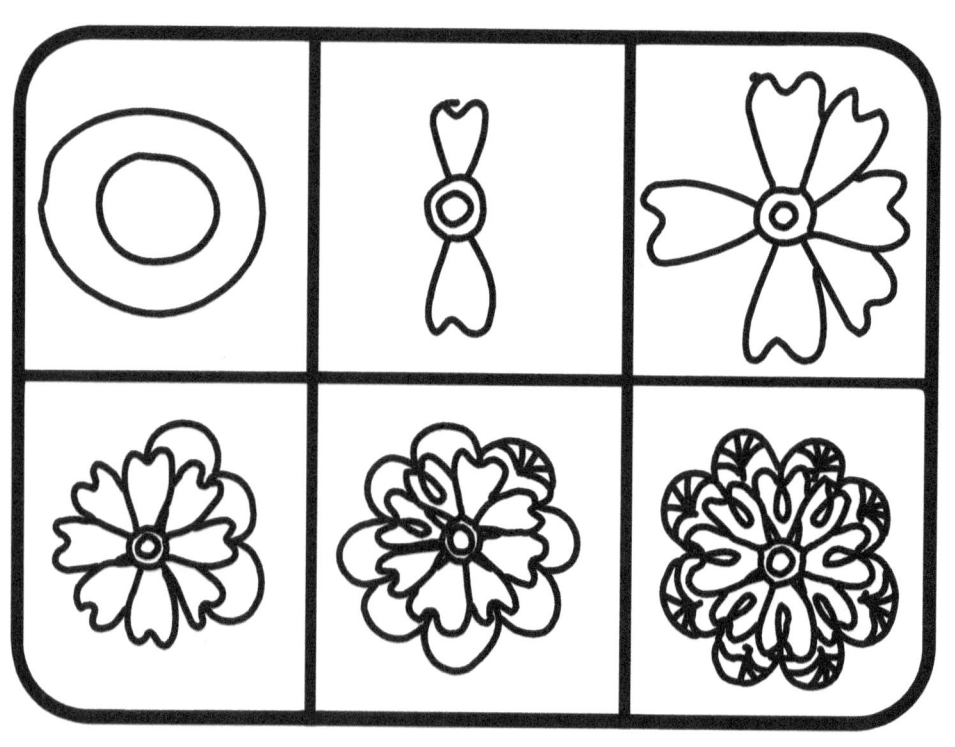

D

DecoLoop-Flower

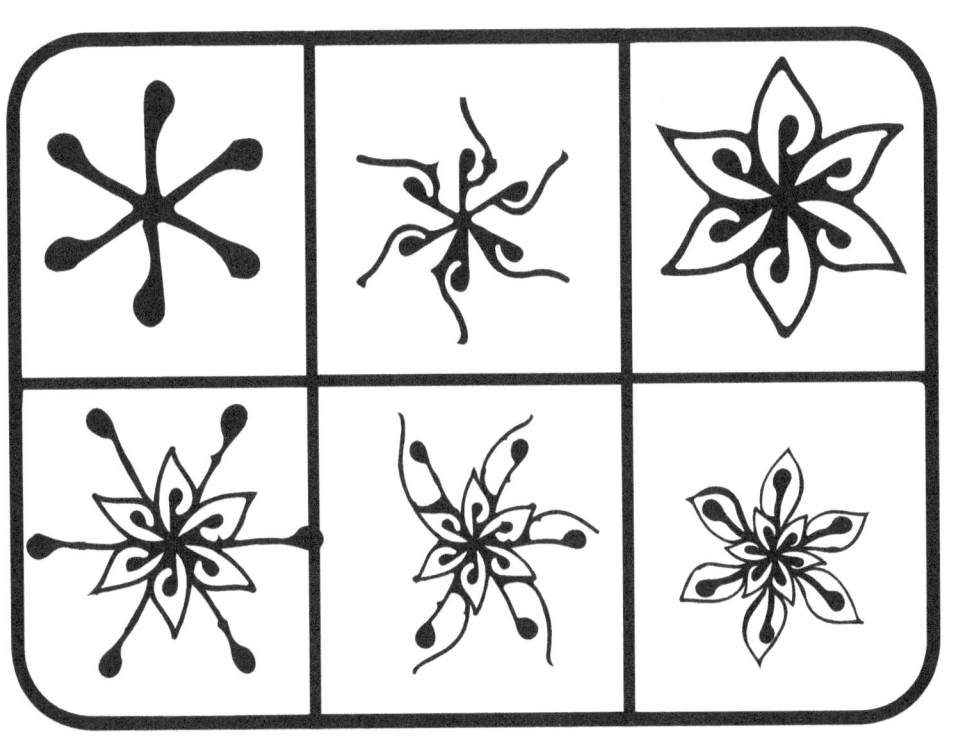

E Everlasting

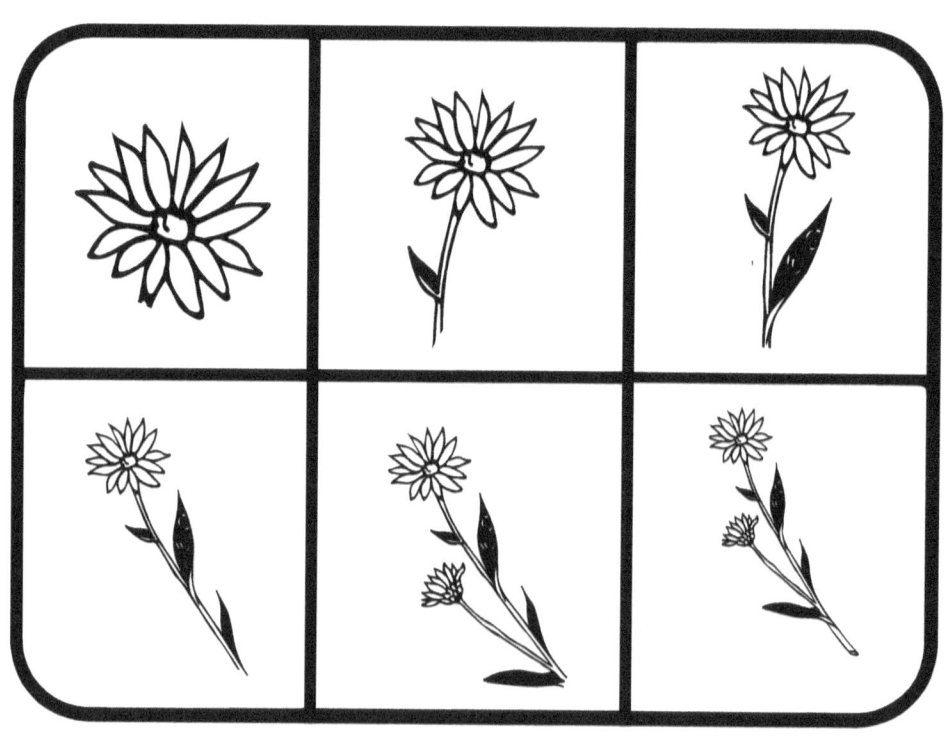

E EightDala

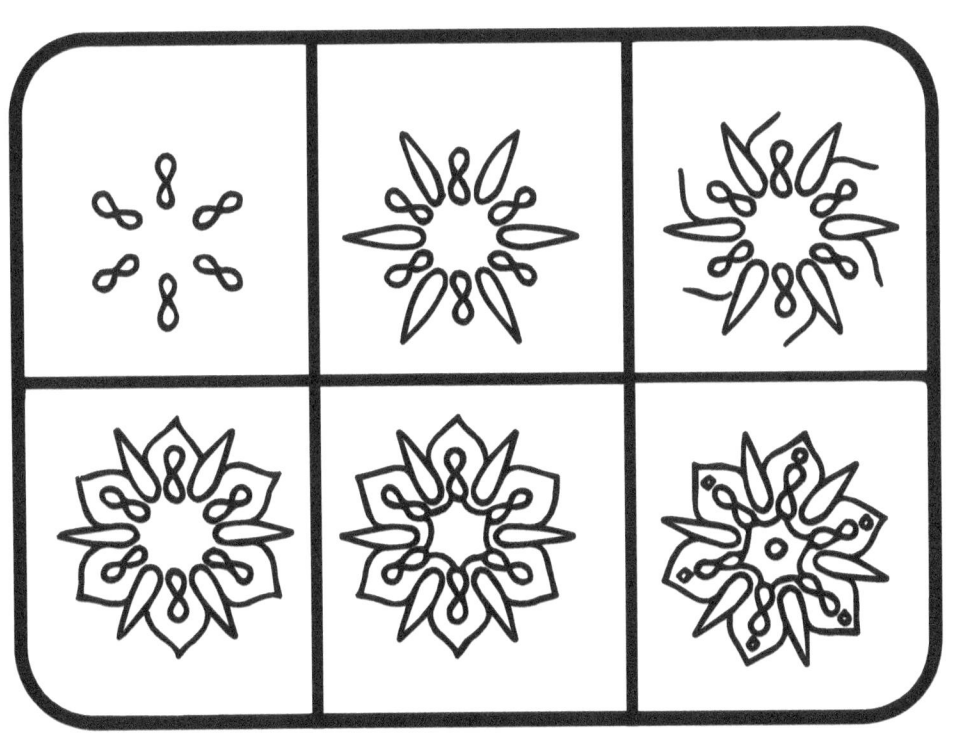

E Eternal

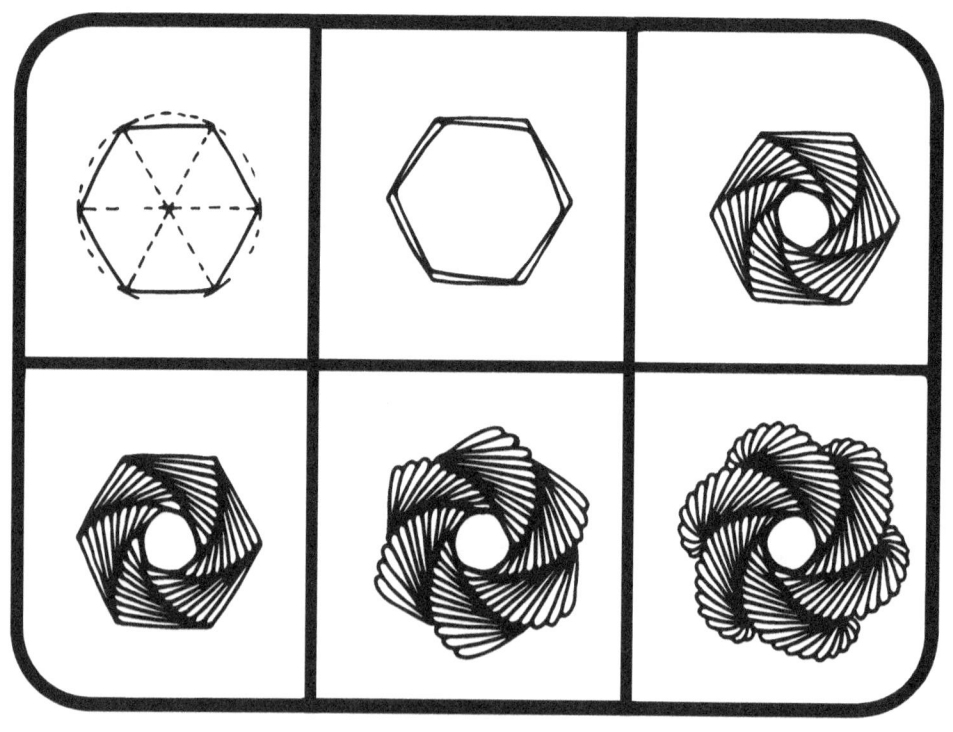

E Enchanted

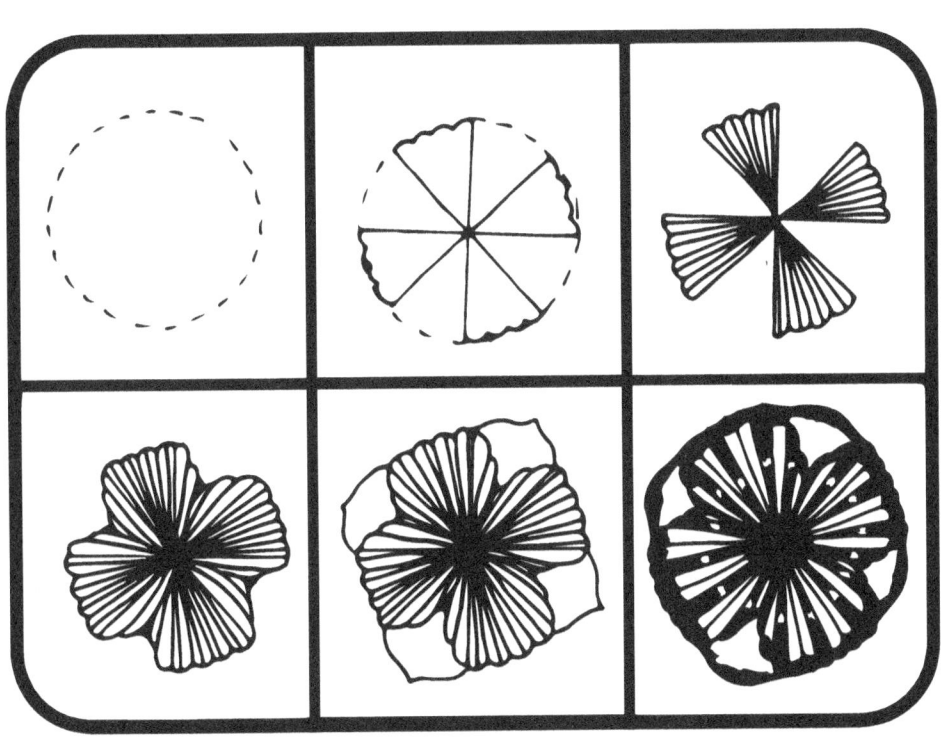

E Ewalu

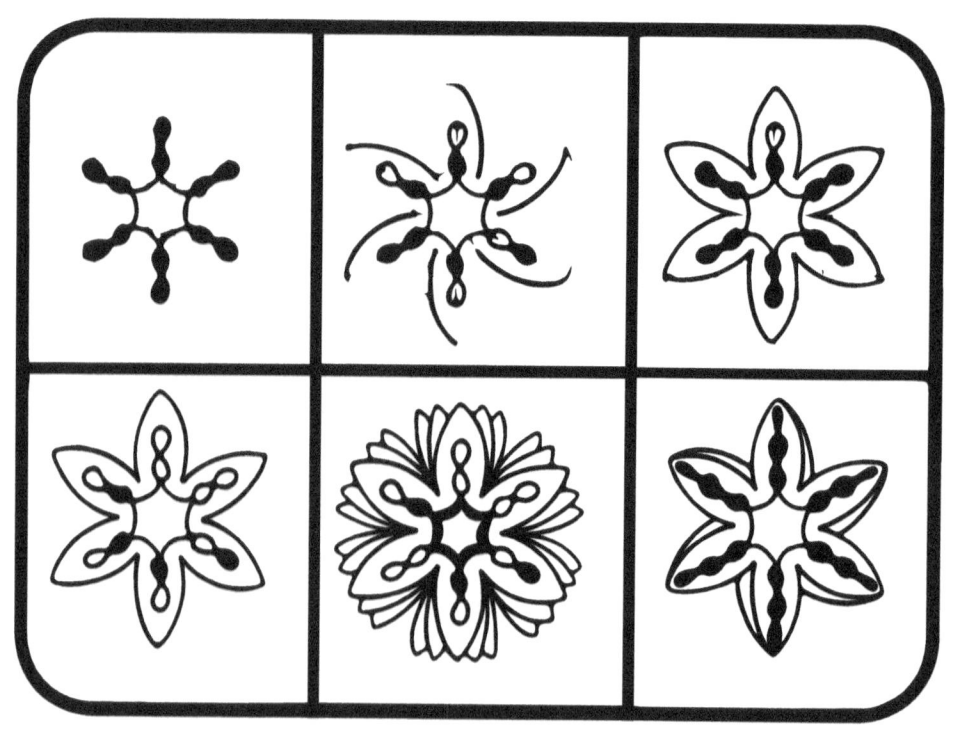

F Foxglove

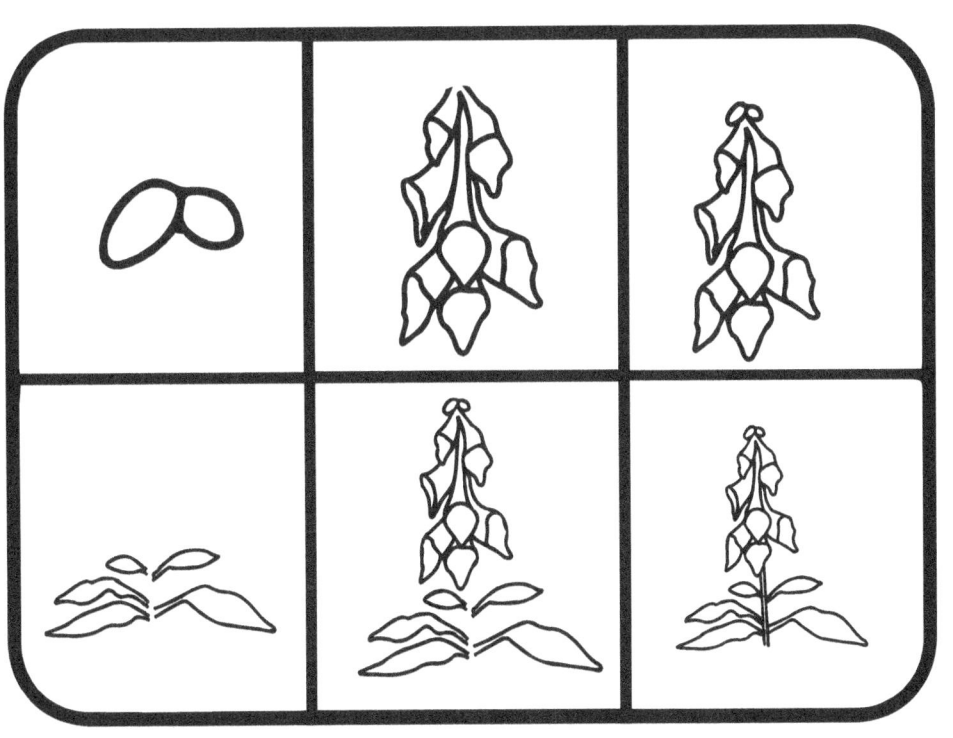

F
Flower Rosy

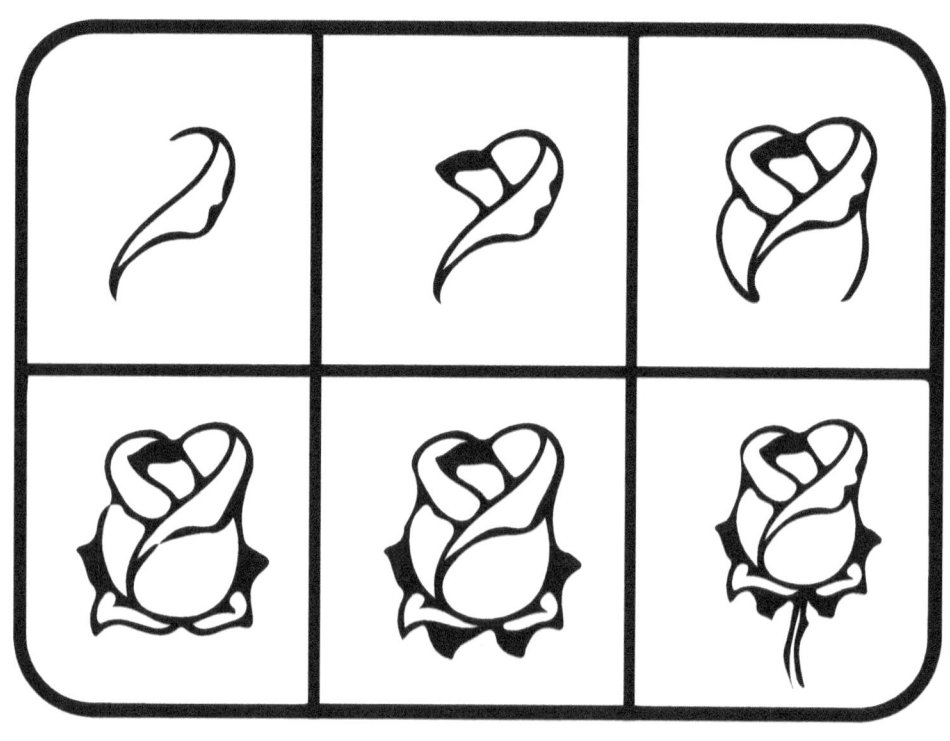

F Fan-Blades

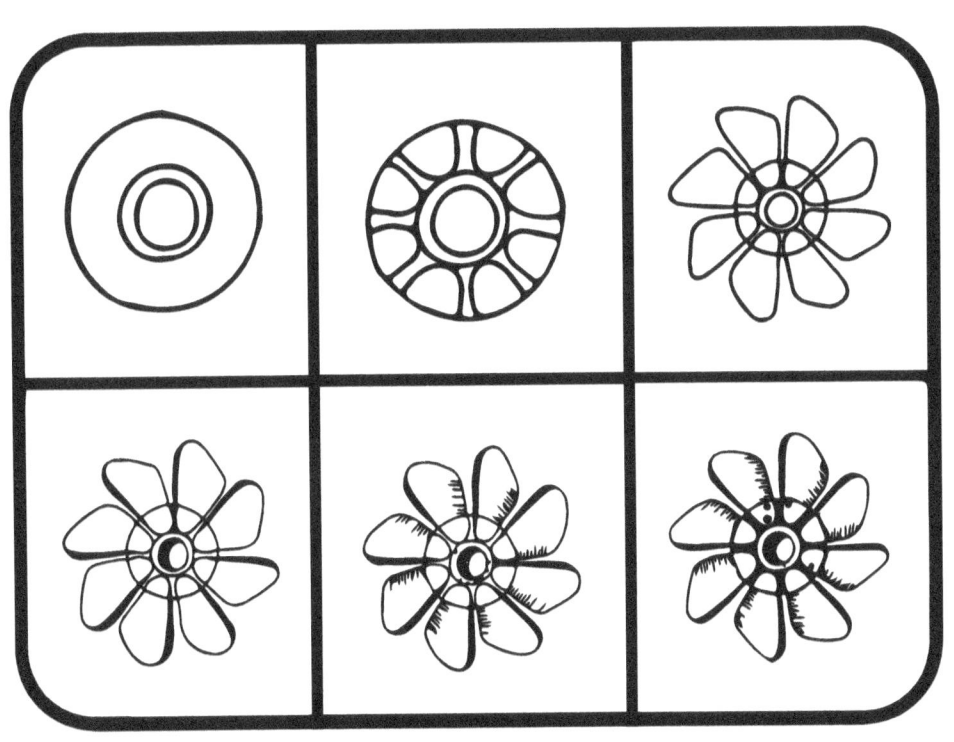

F Fayz

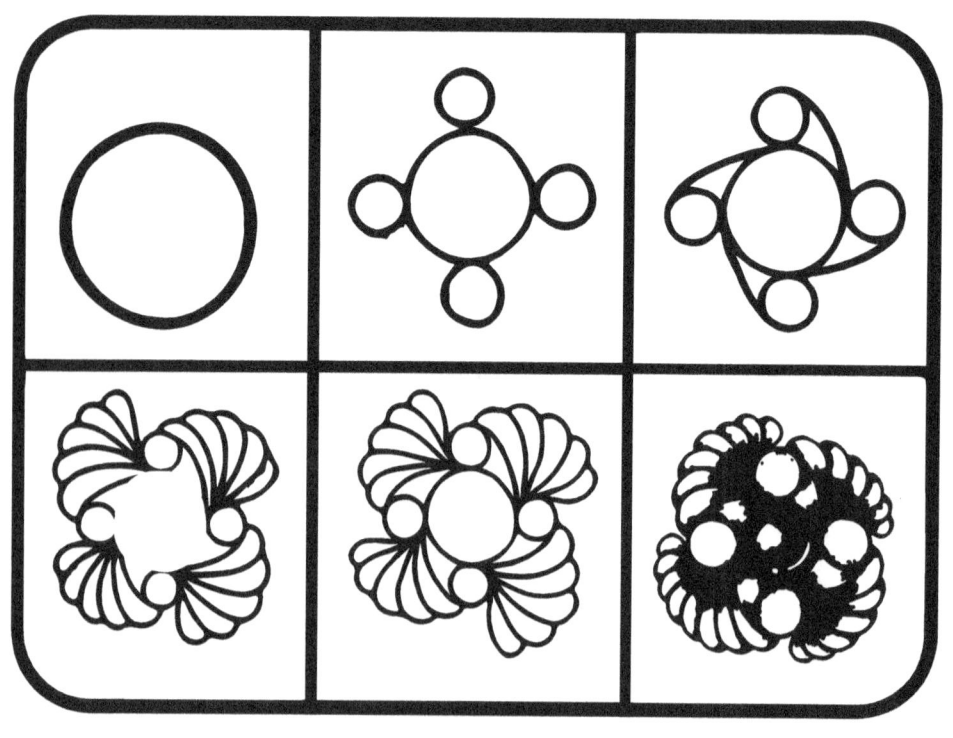

F

Feria

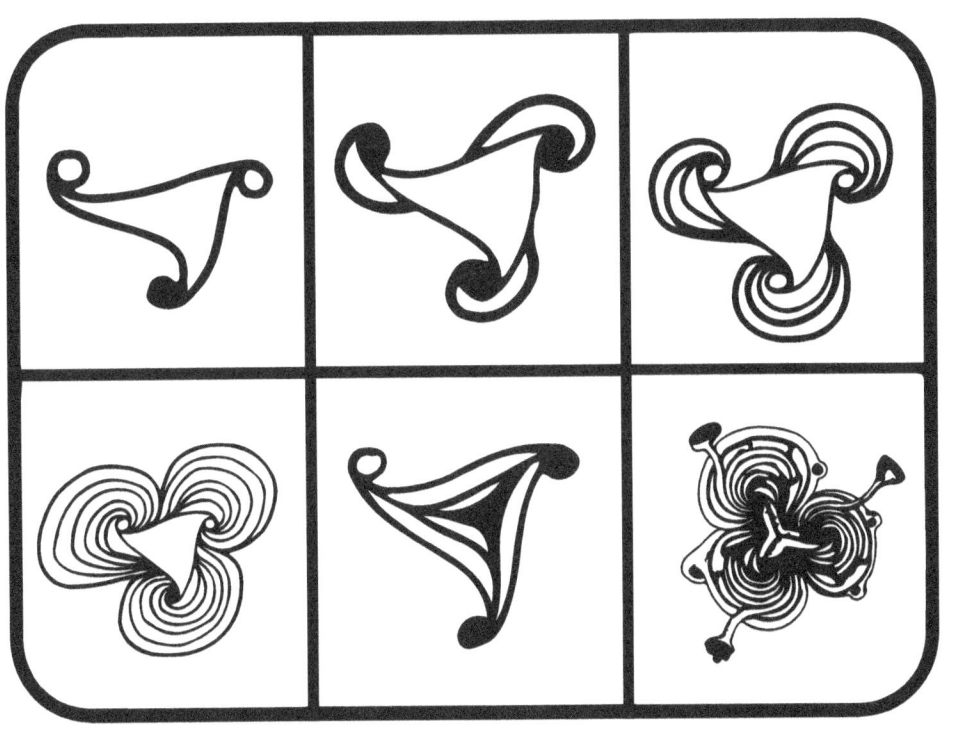

F

Flame-flower

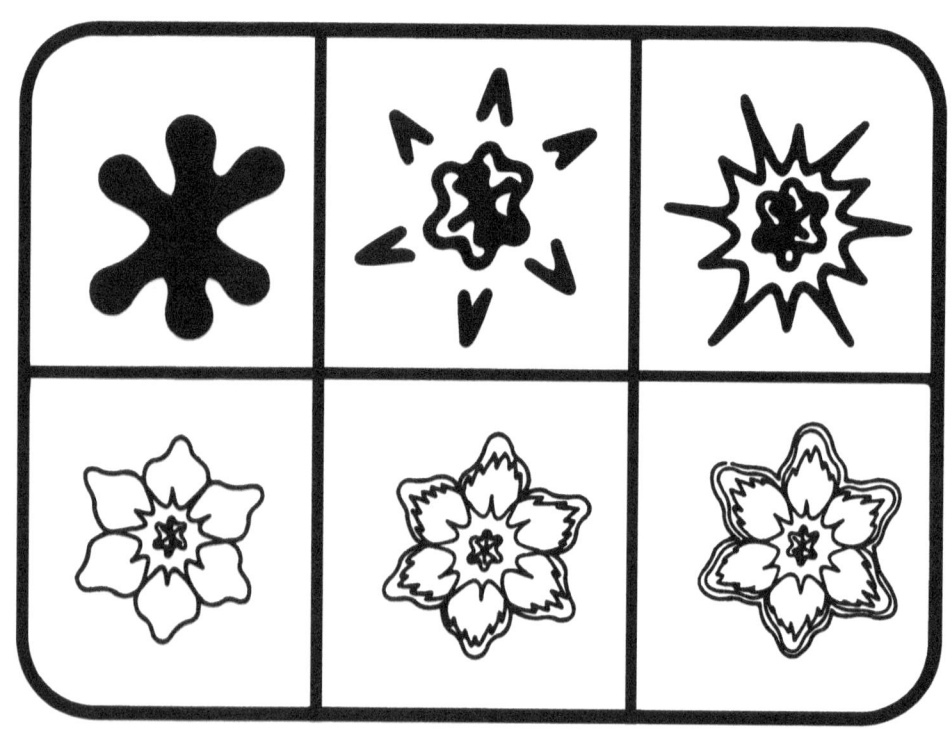

G Geranium

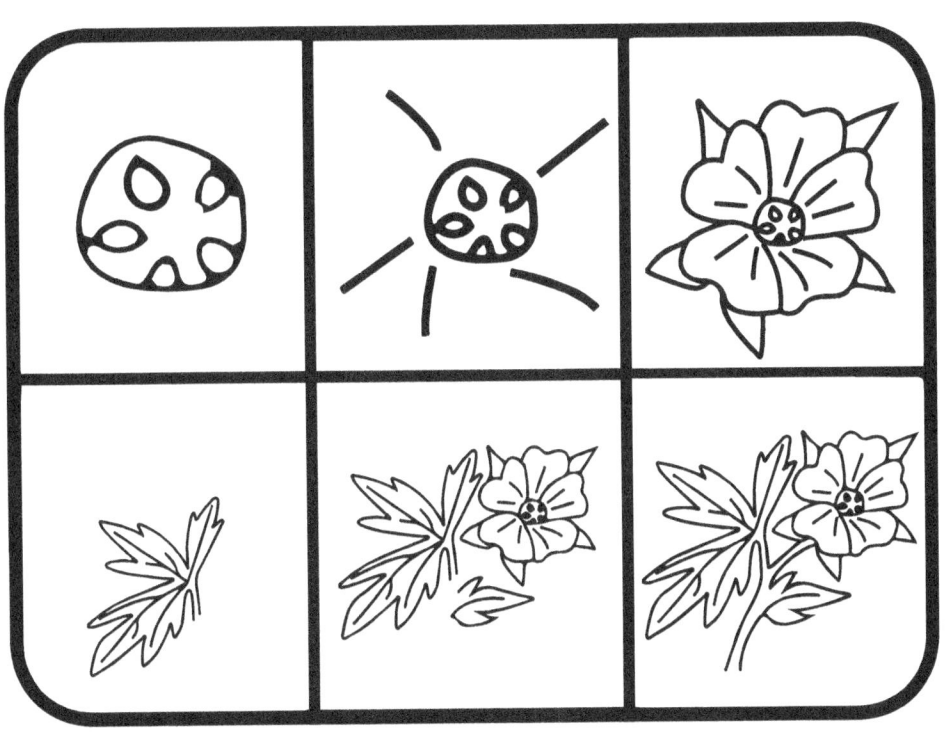

G Glazy

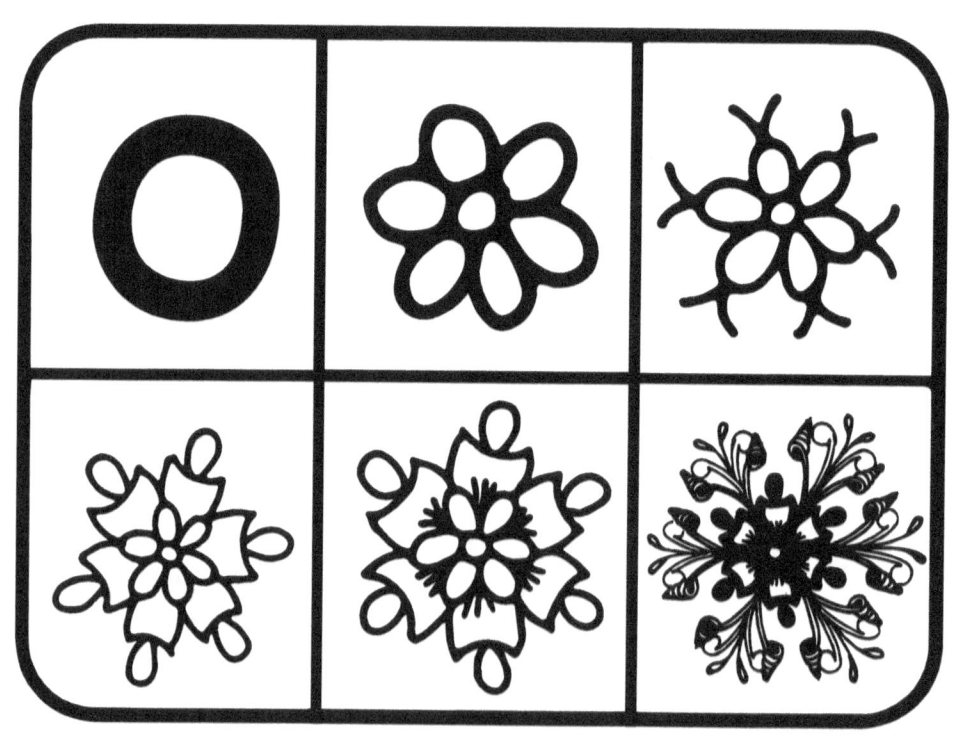

G Gear-Flower

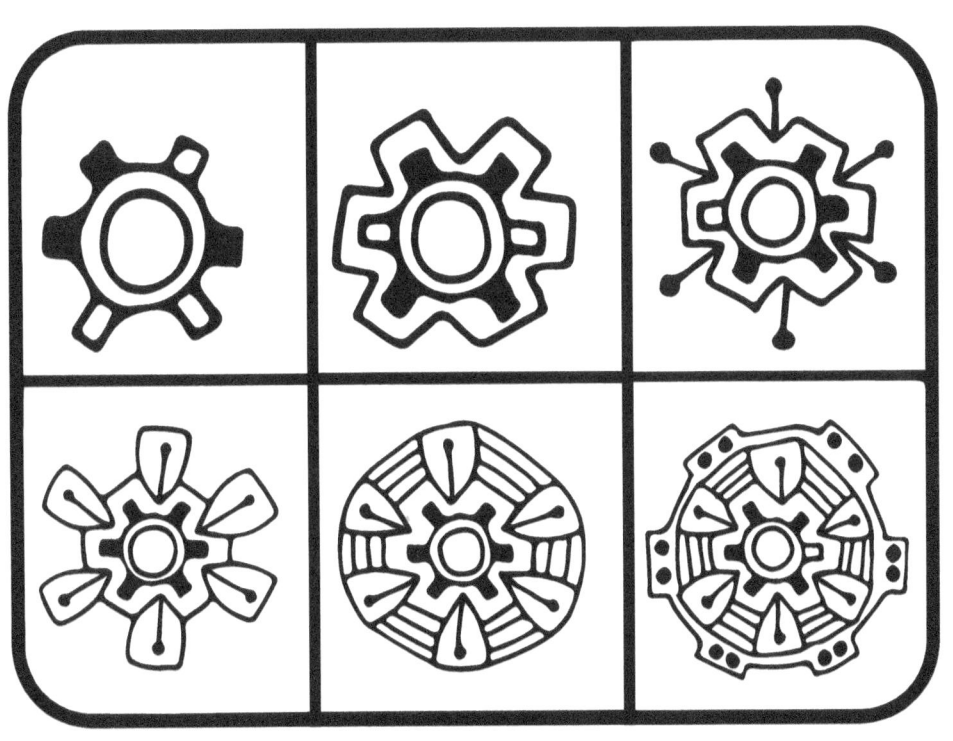

H Honeysuckle

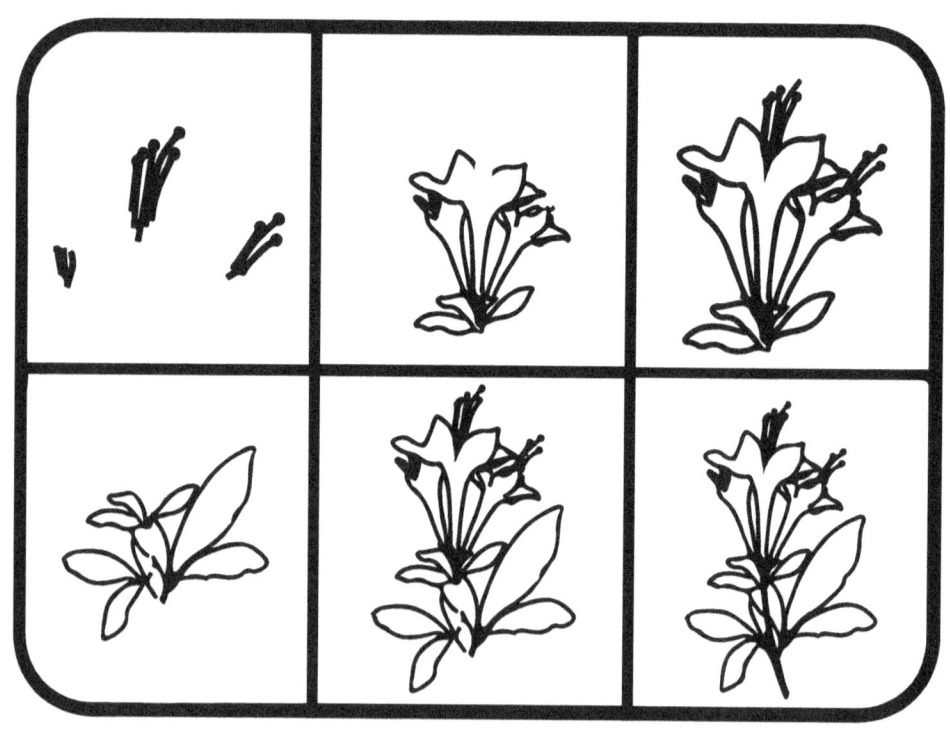

H Hyacinth

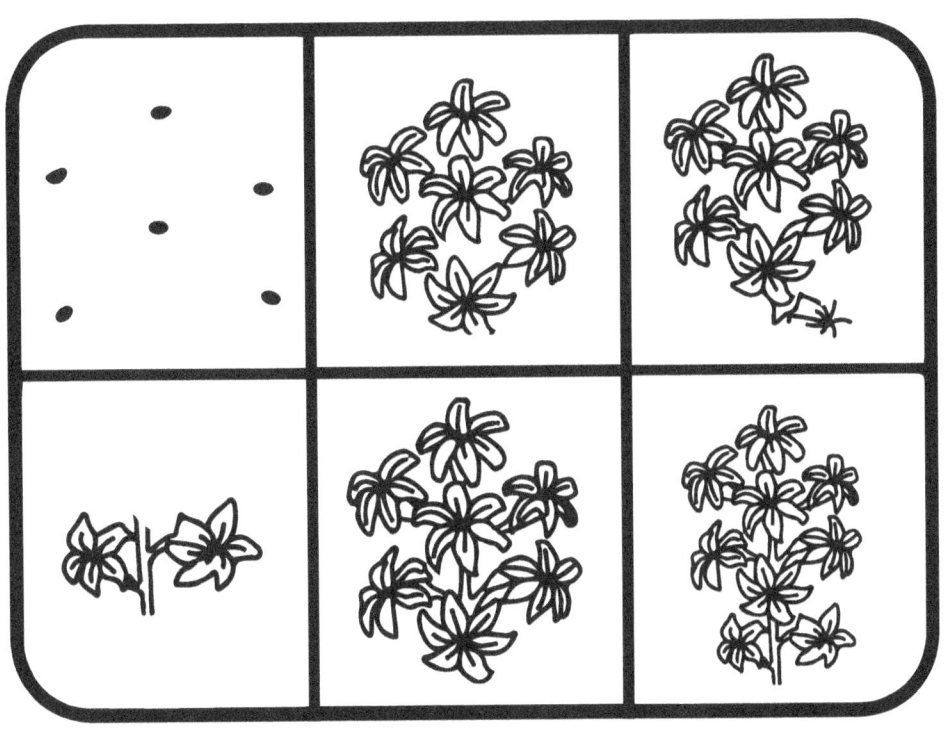

H Hamsix-Flor

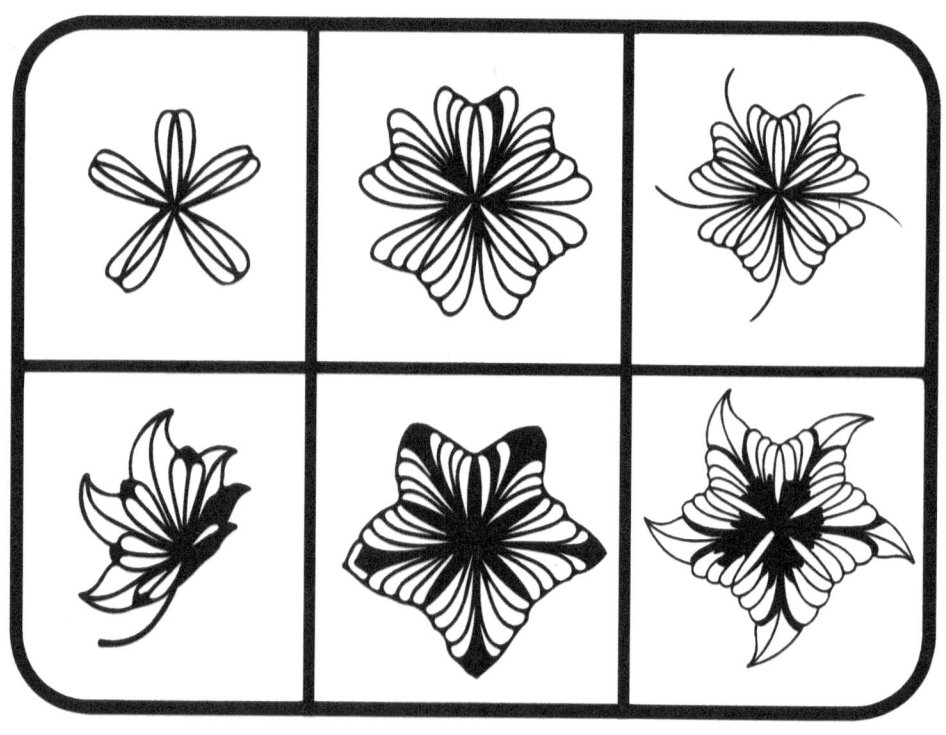

H HeartStar

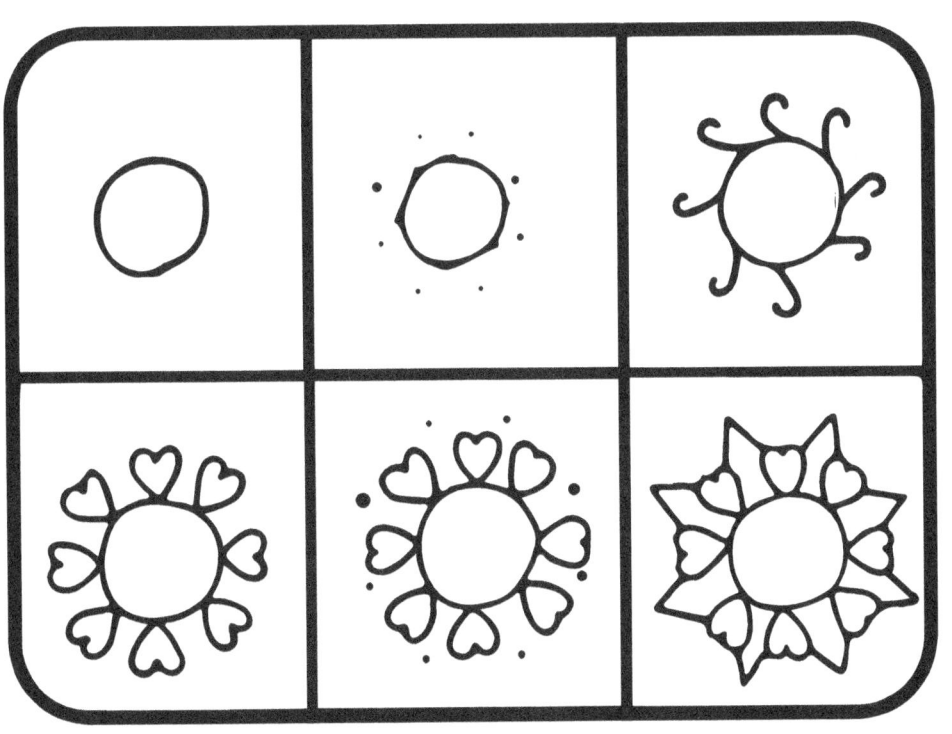

H Hearts-Apart

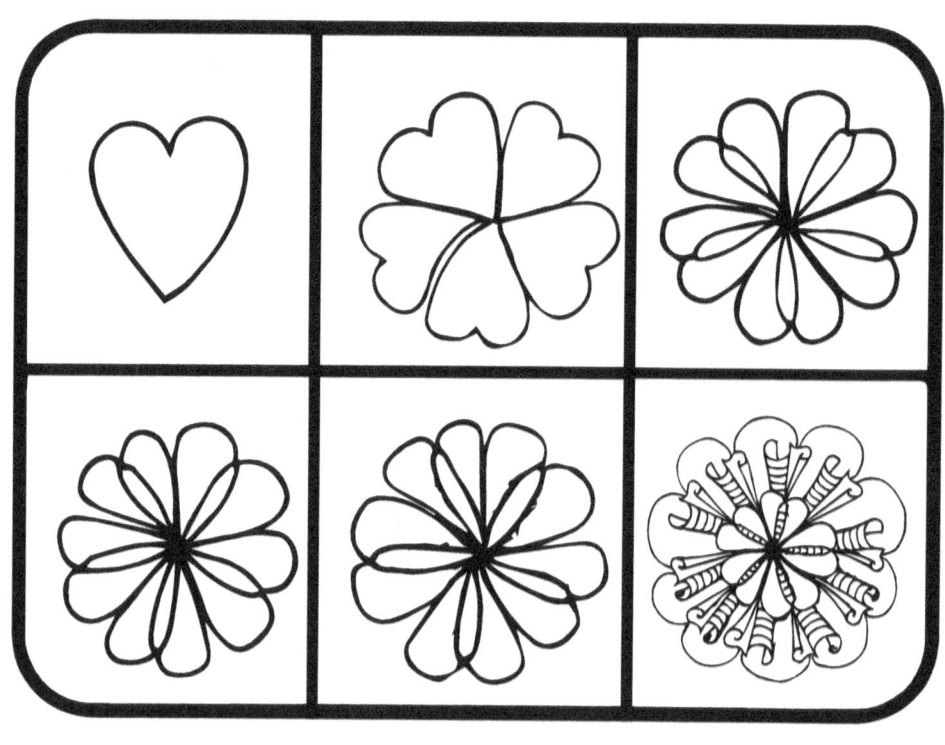

I Iris

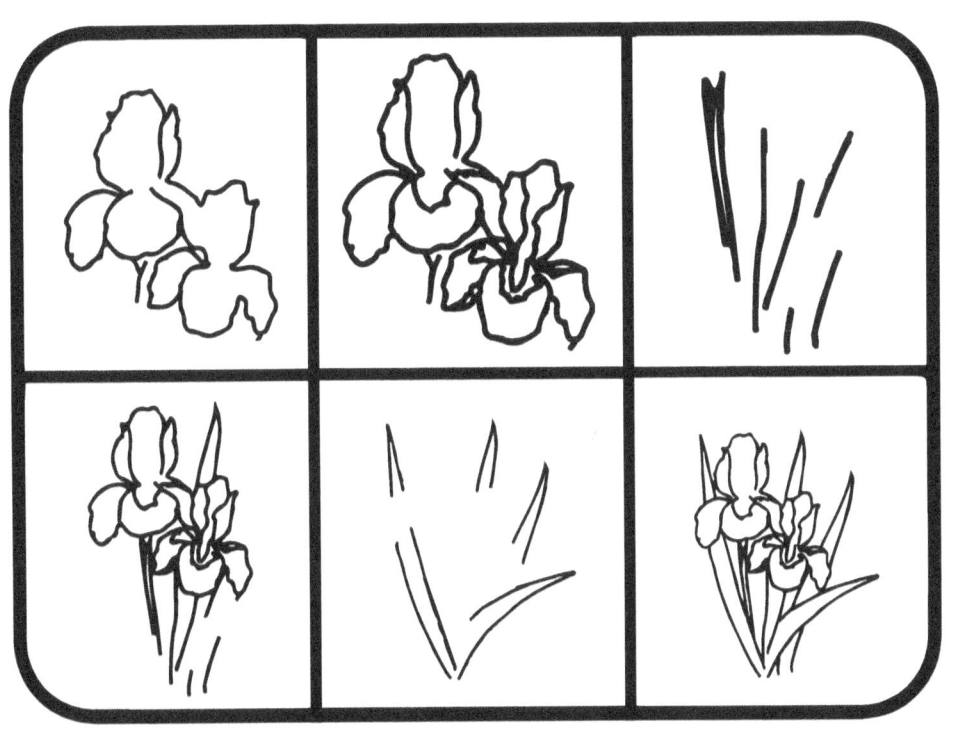

I
Iva

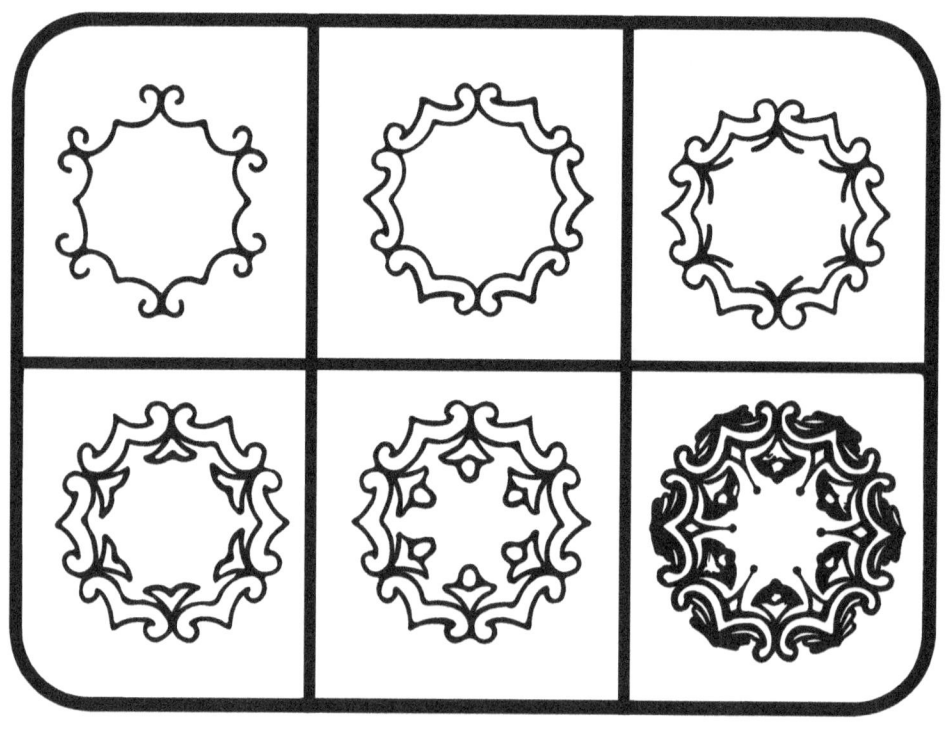

I Ixia

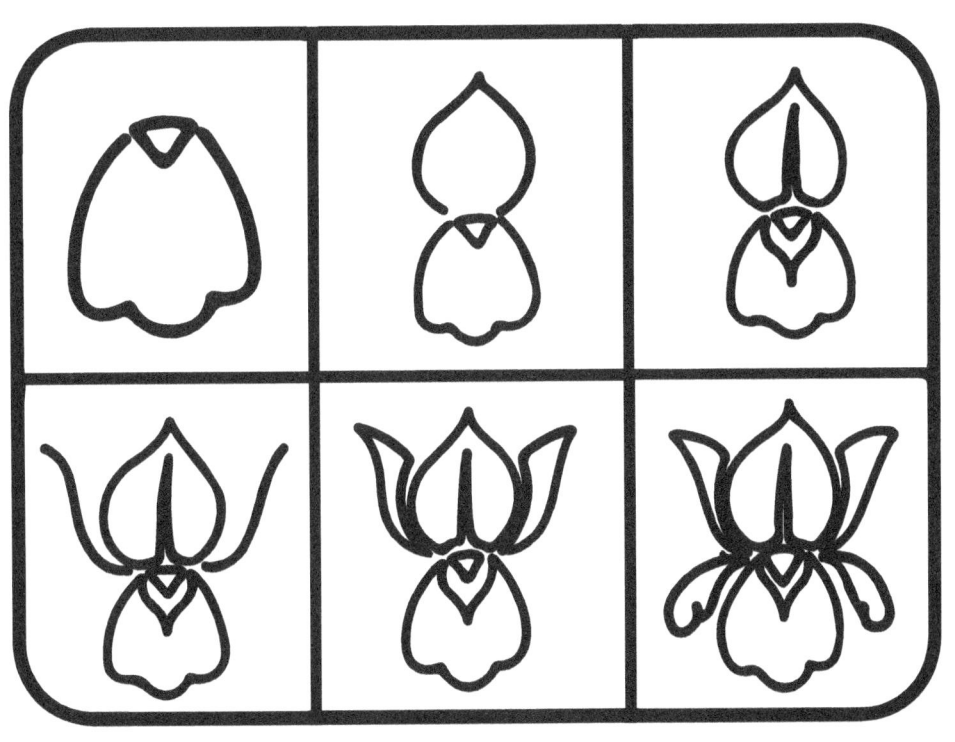

J

Jonquil

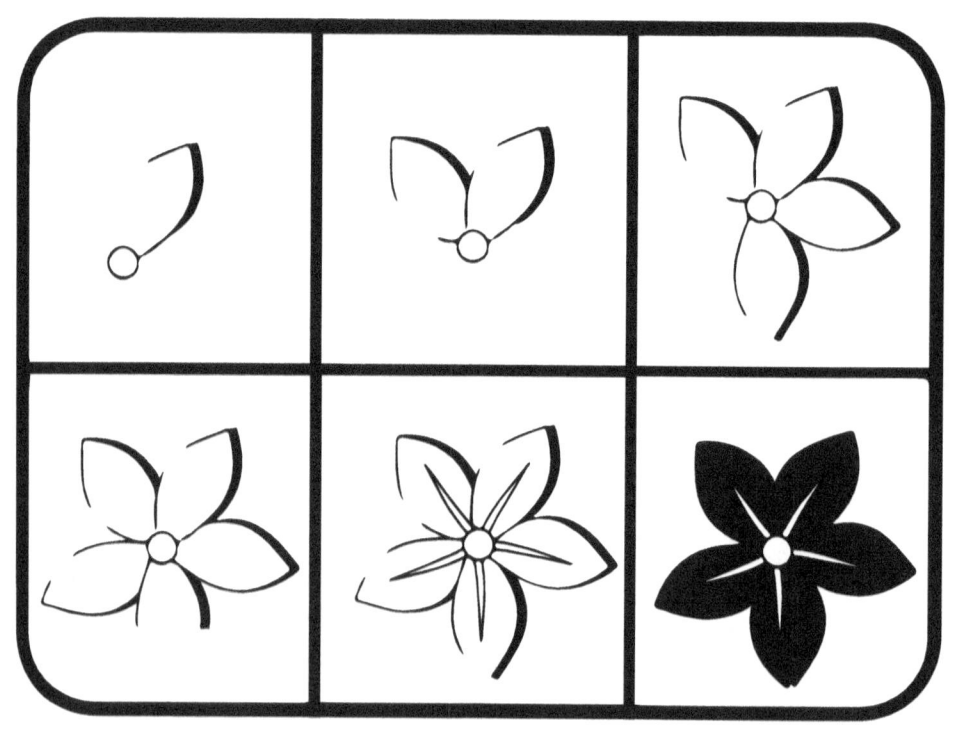

J

Jester

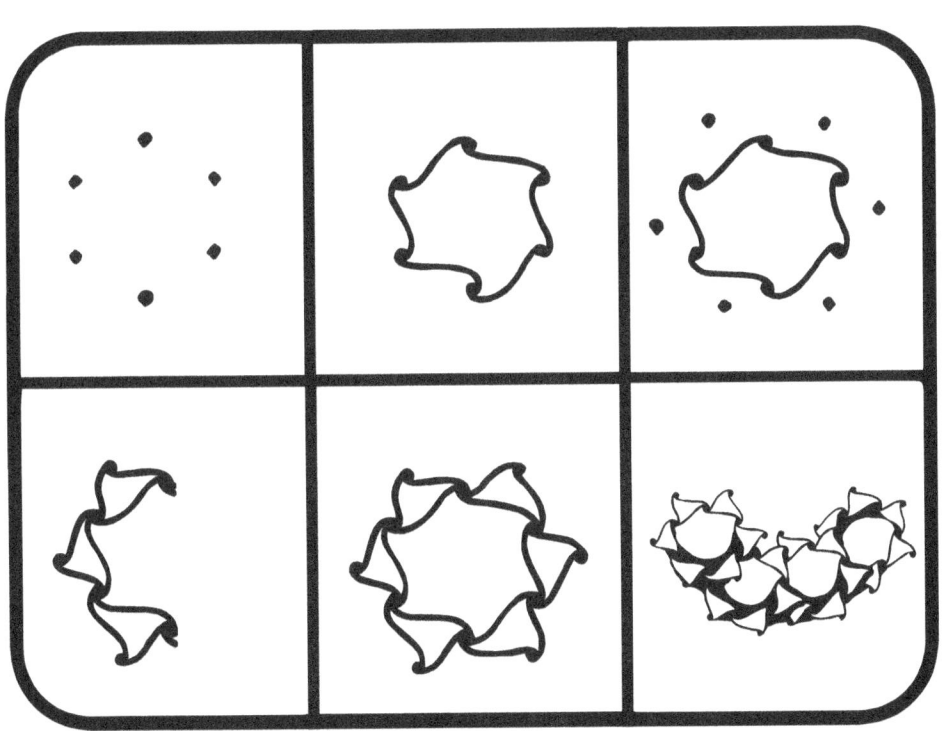

J

Jiami

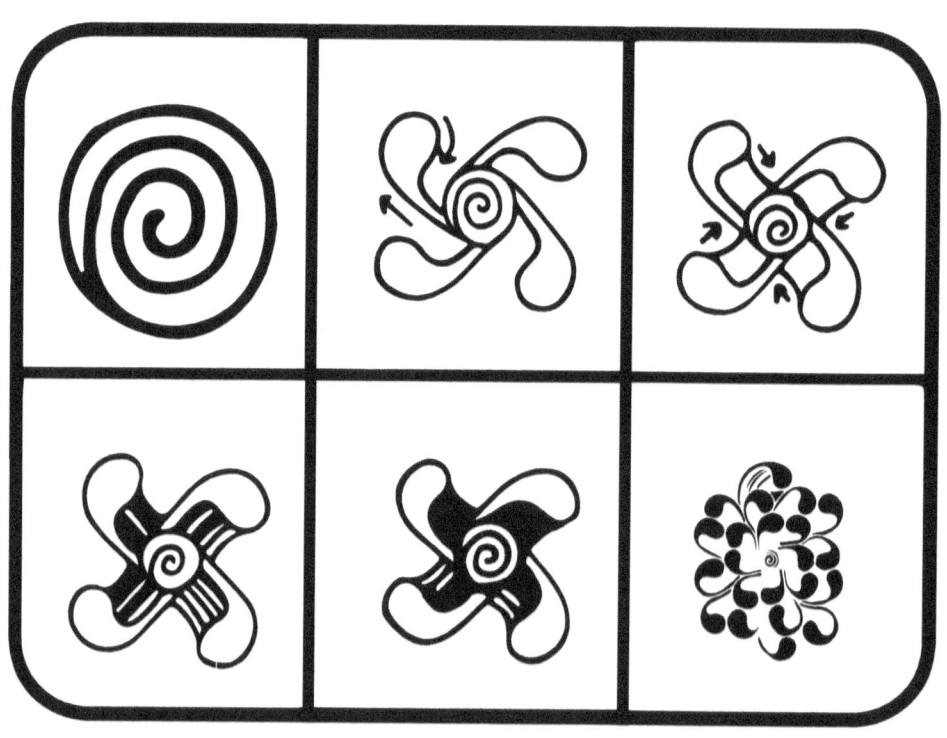

K Kalmia

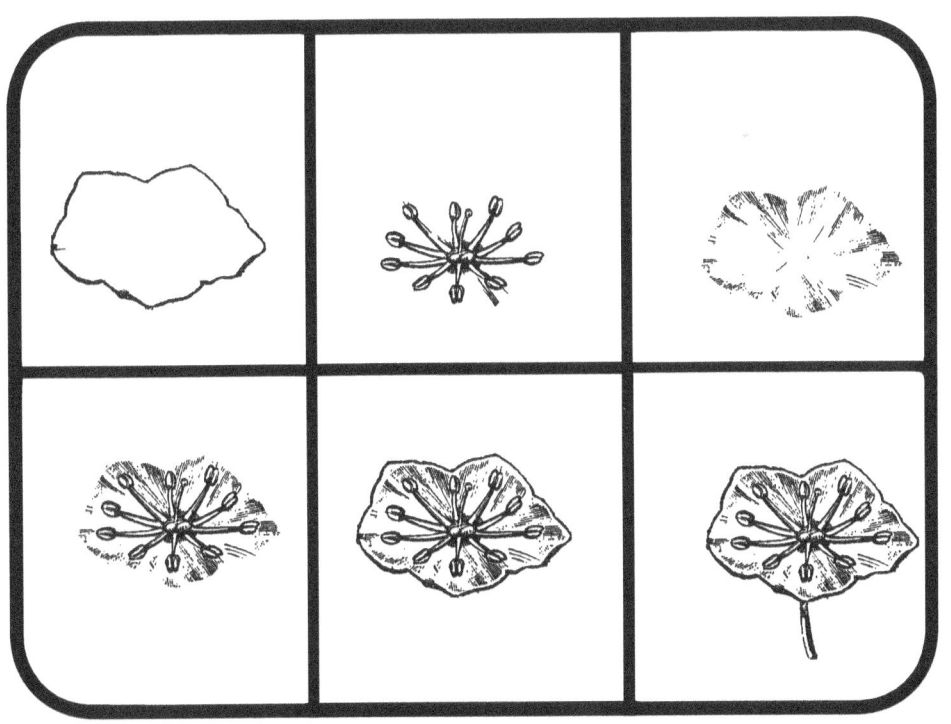

K KaroFlo

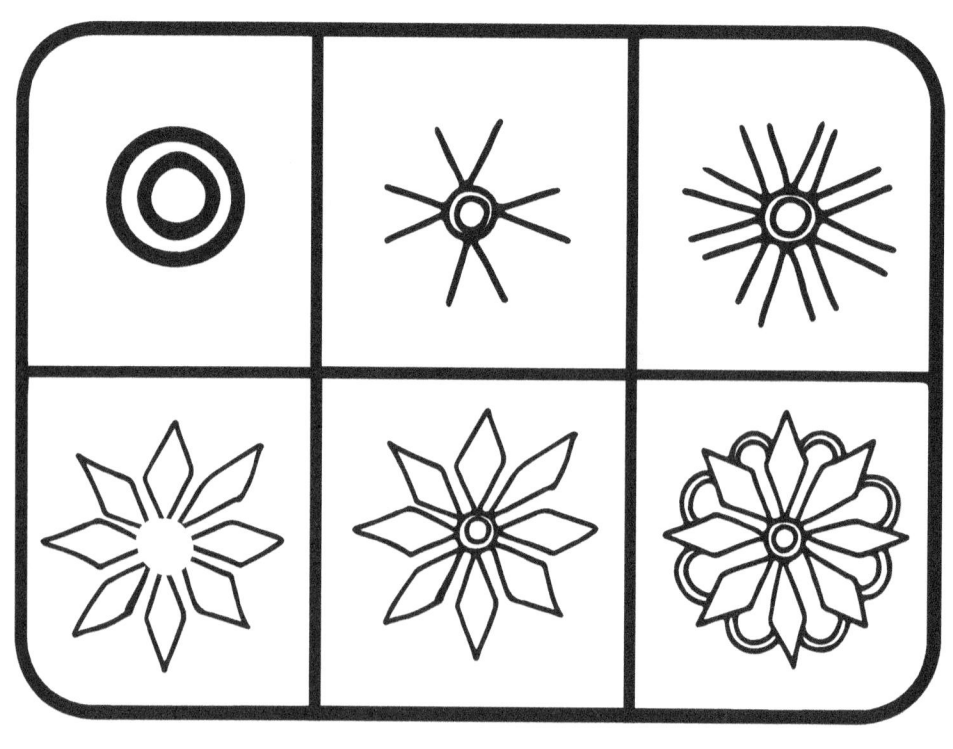

K Khloma

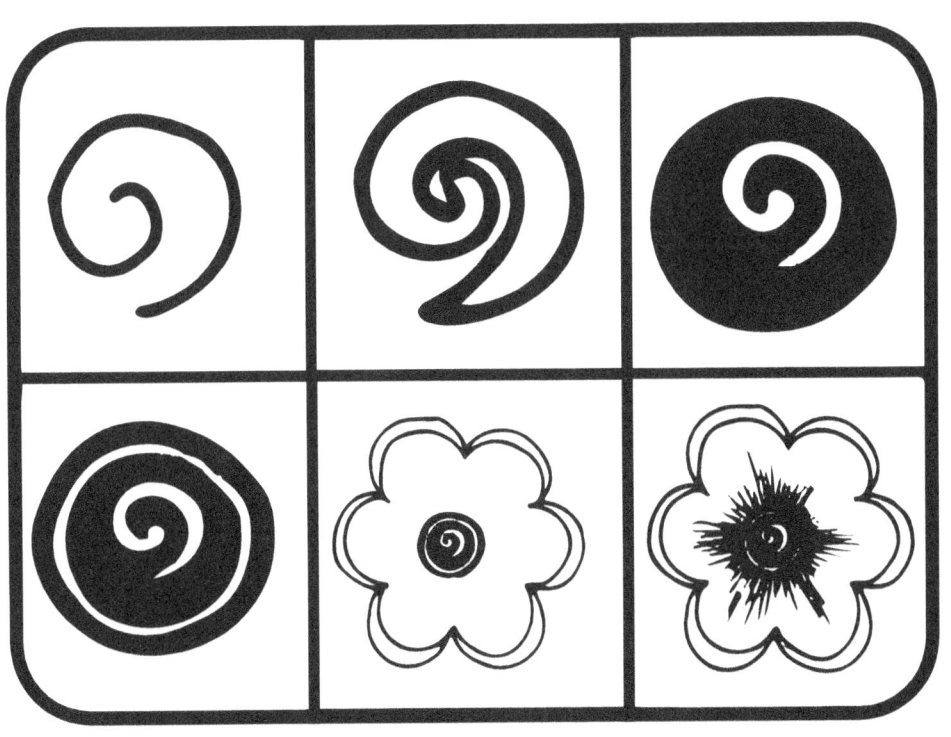

K Kiki

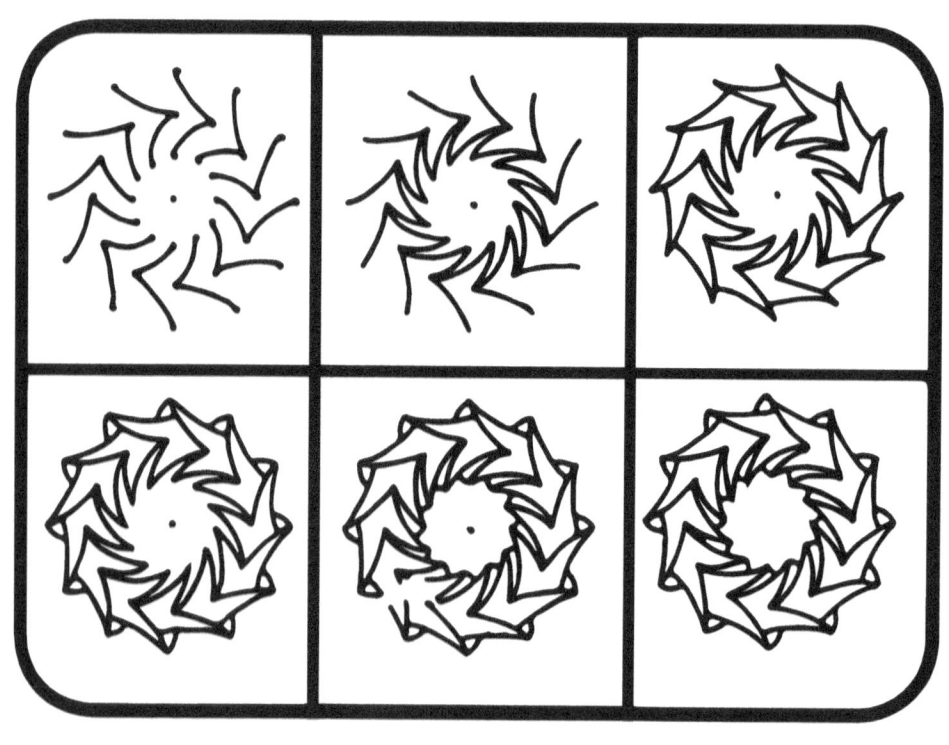

L Larkspur

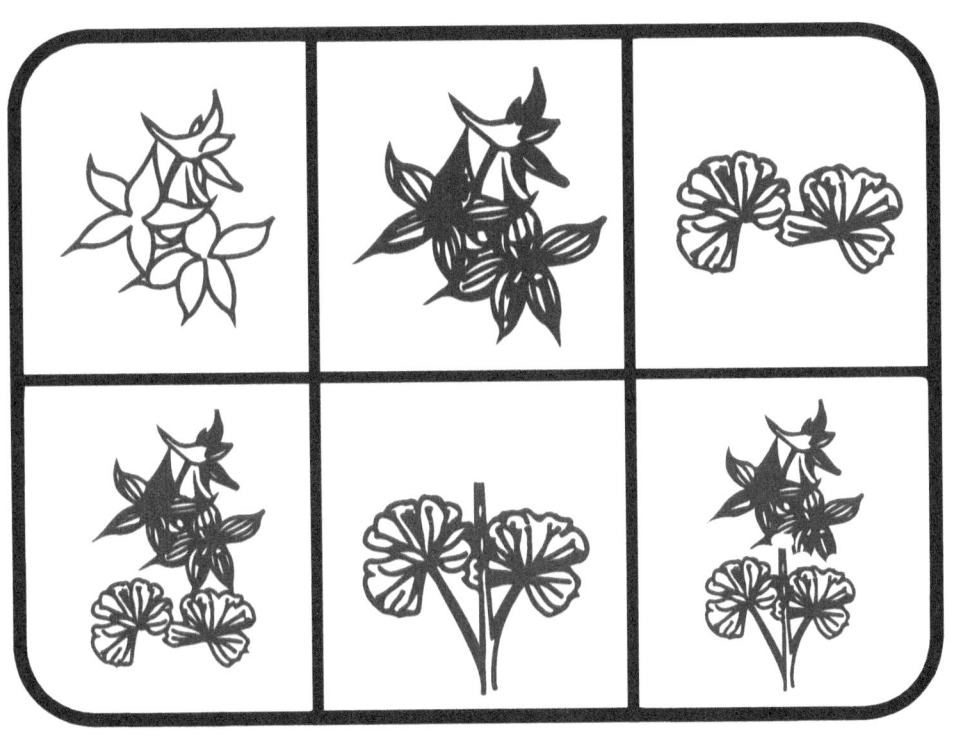

L Lavender

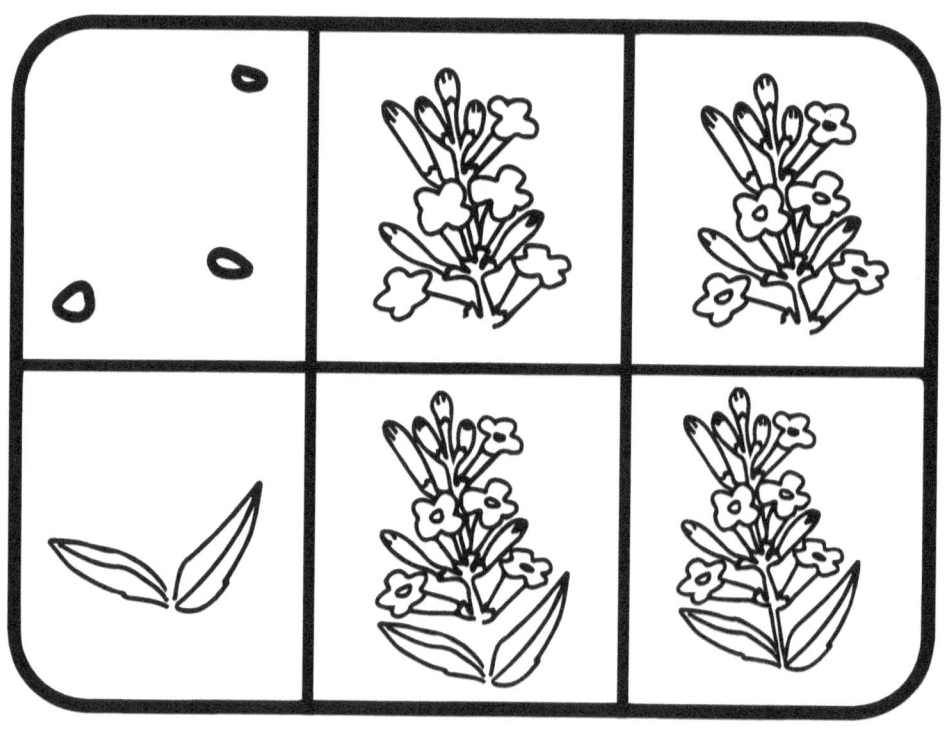

L Lilac

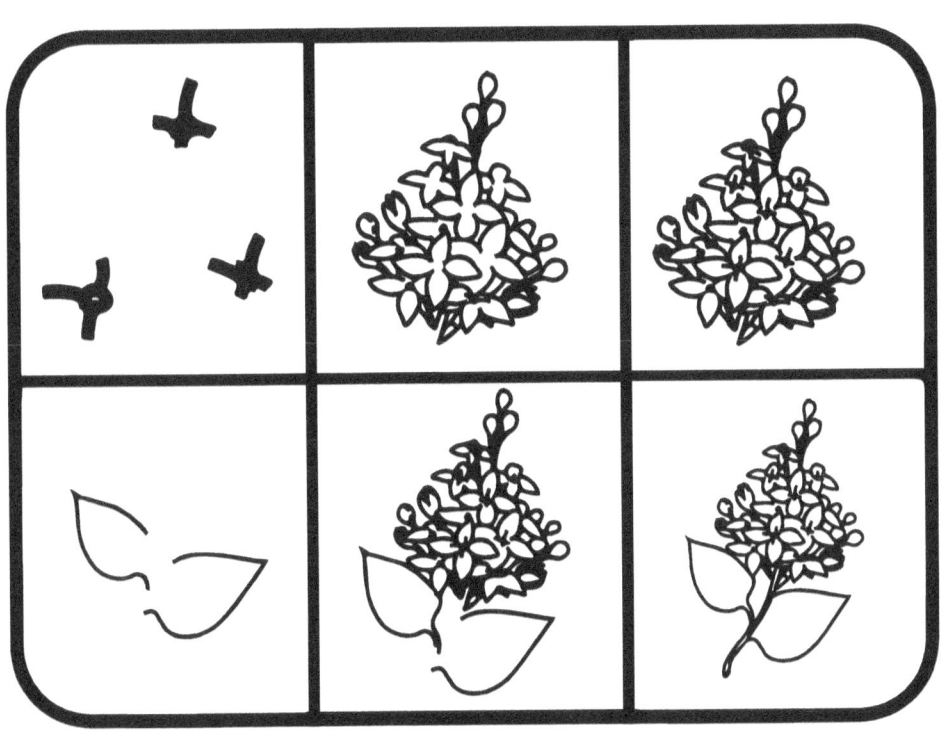

L Lily

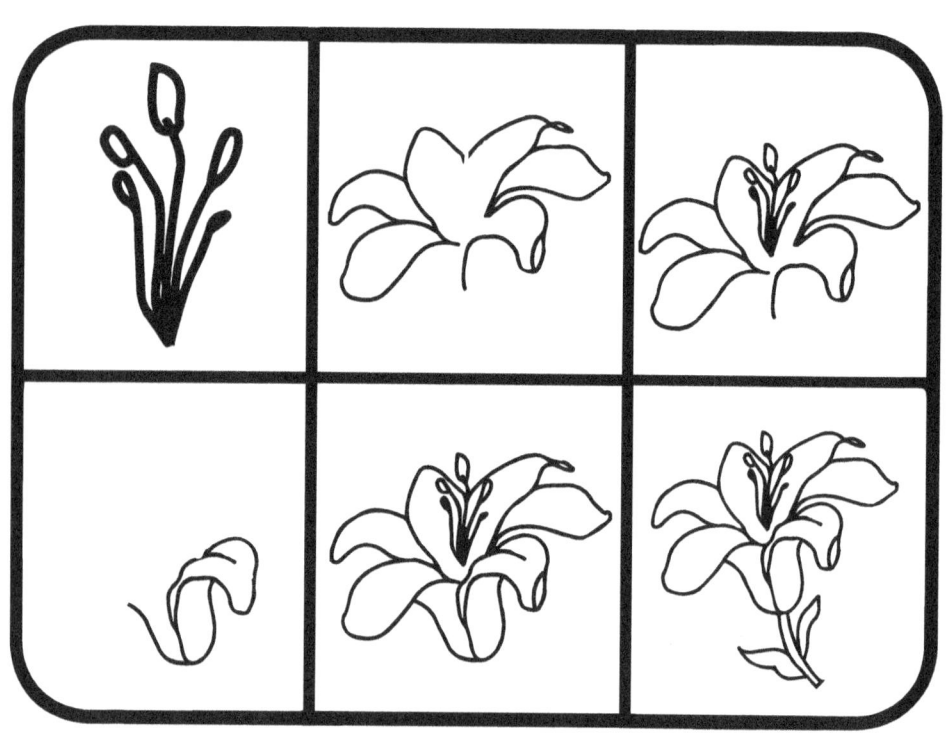

L Lotus Flower

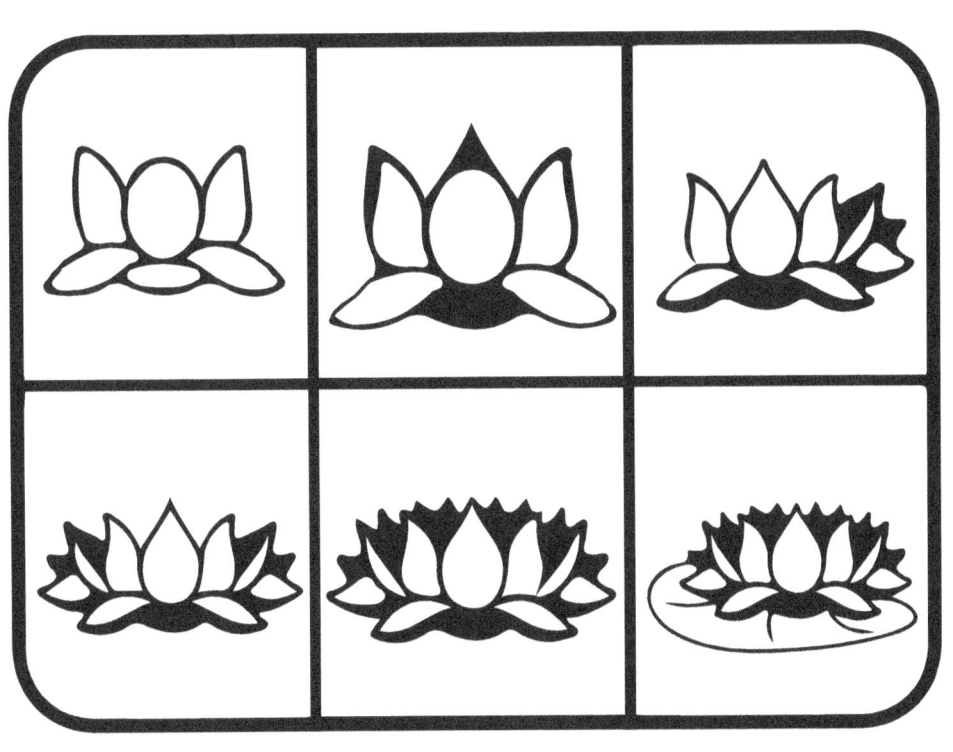

L Laflor

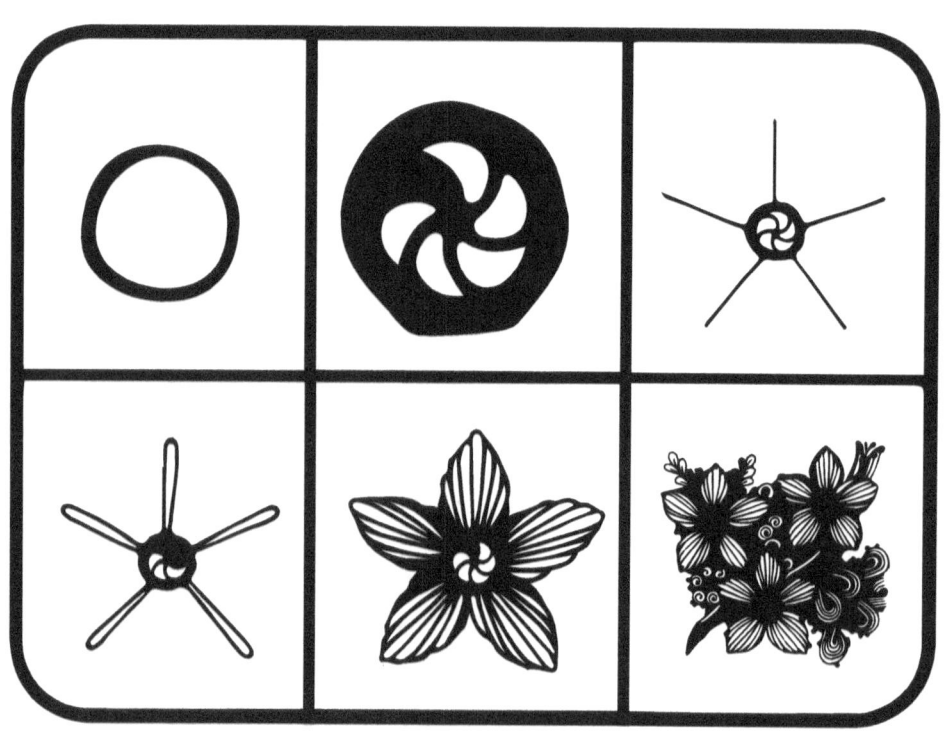

L Loopfill

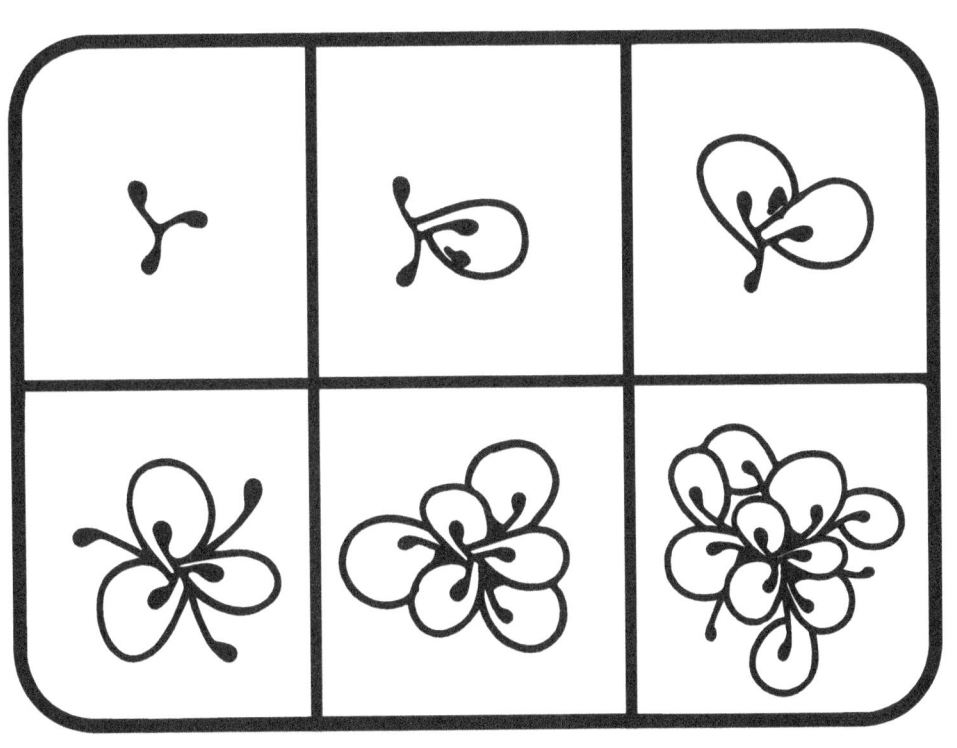

L Luheart

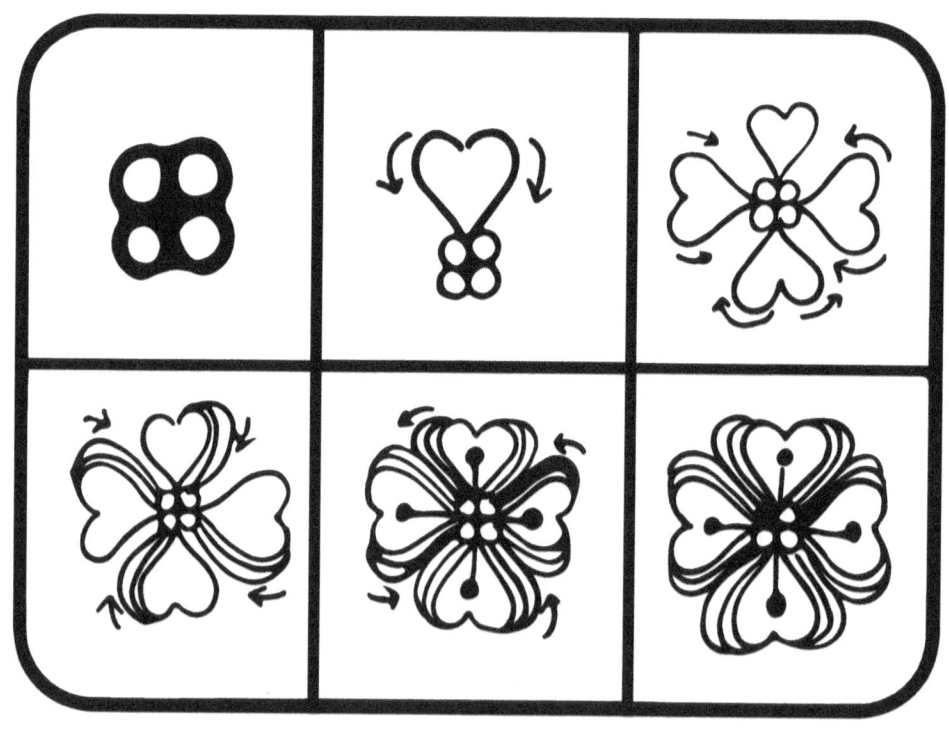

M Marigold

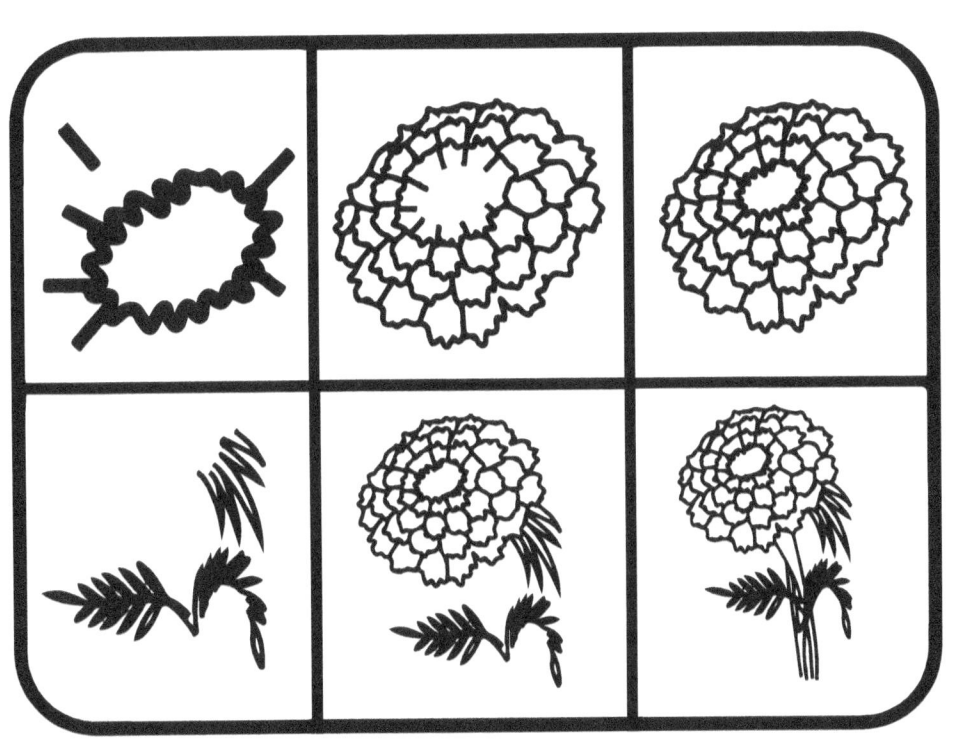

M Margarita

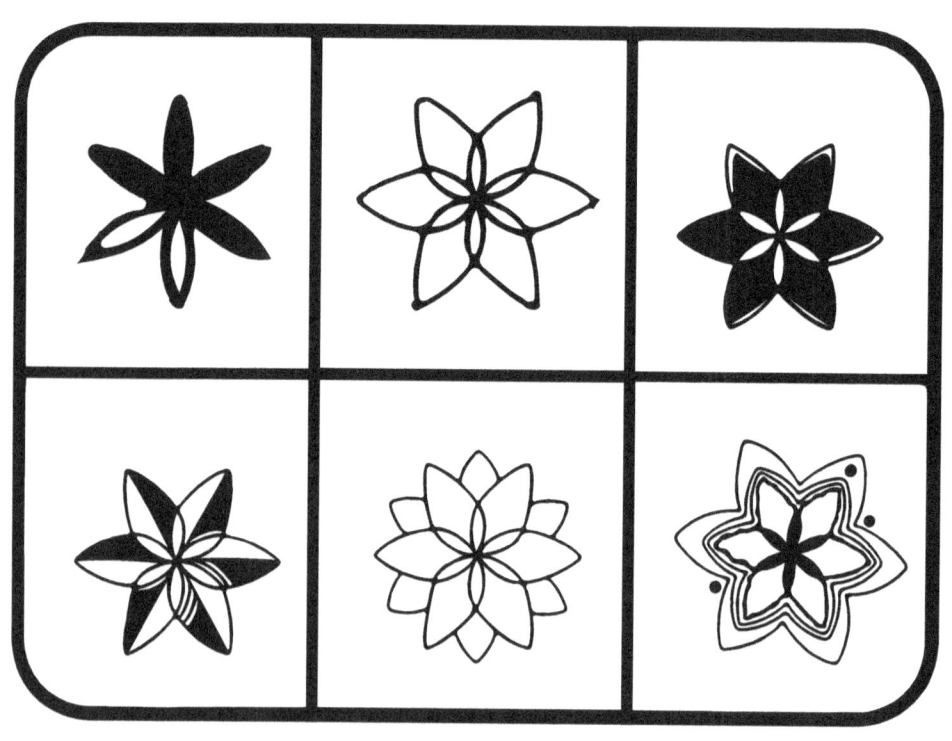

M Mehndi-Bloom

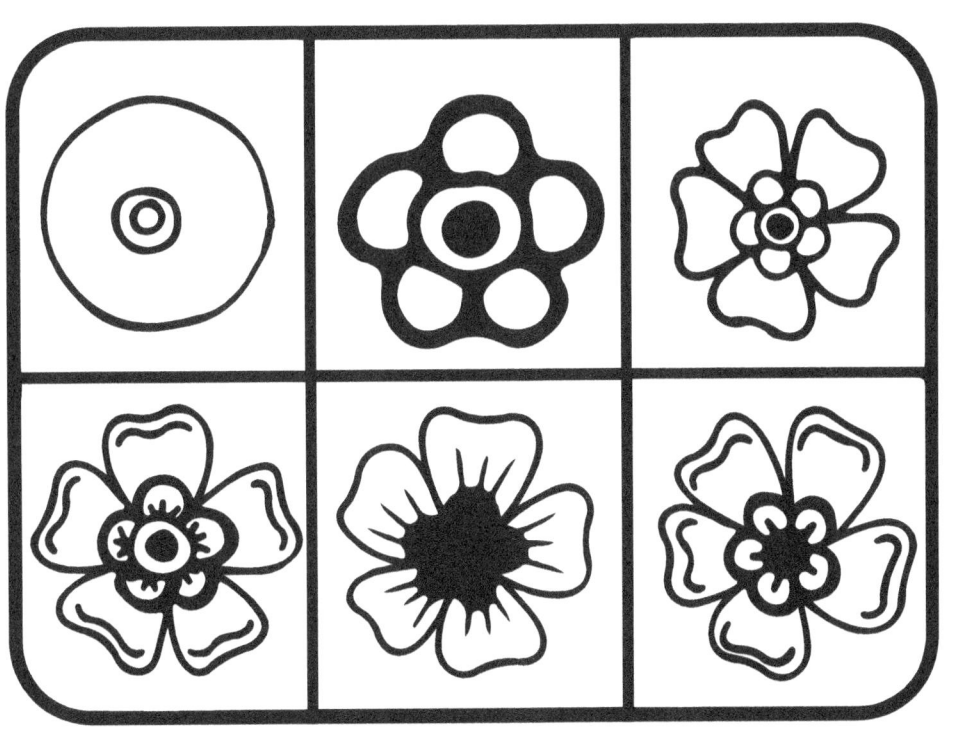

M Mookaflower

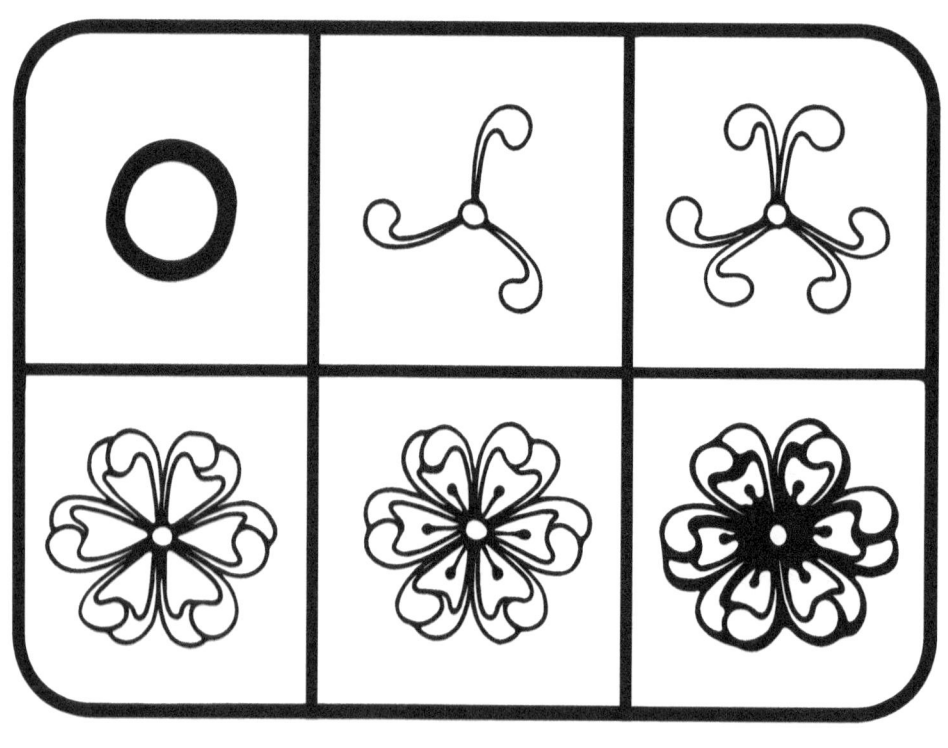

M Muscari

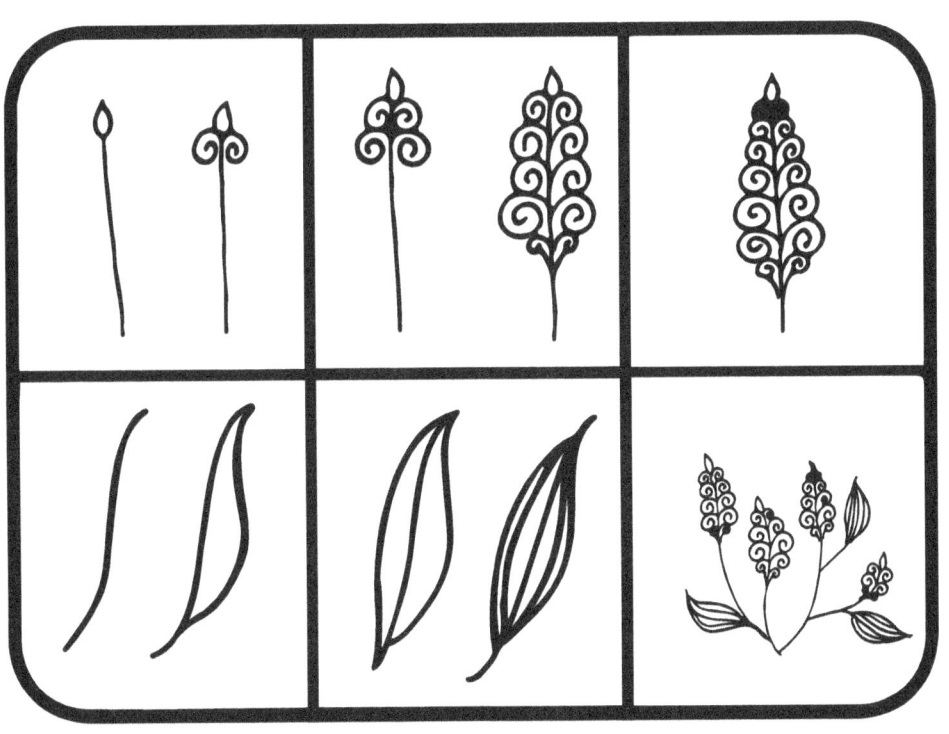

N

Nelli-Kolam

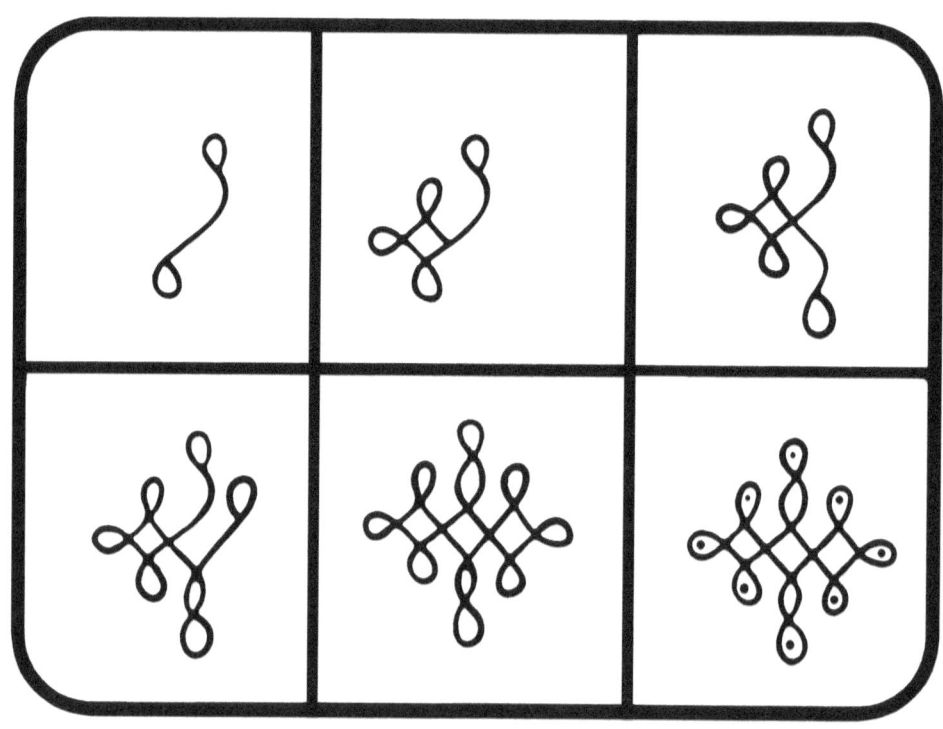

N Narcissus

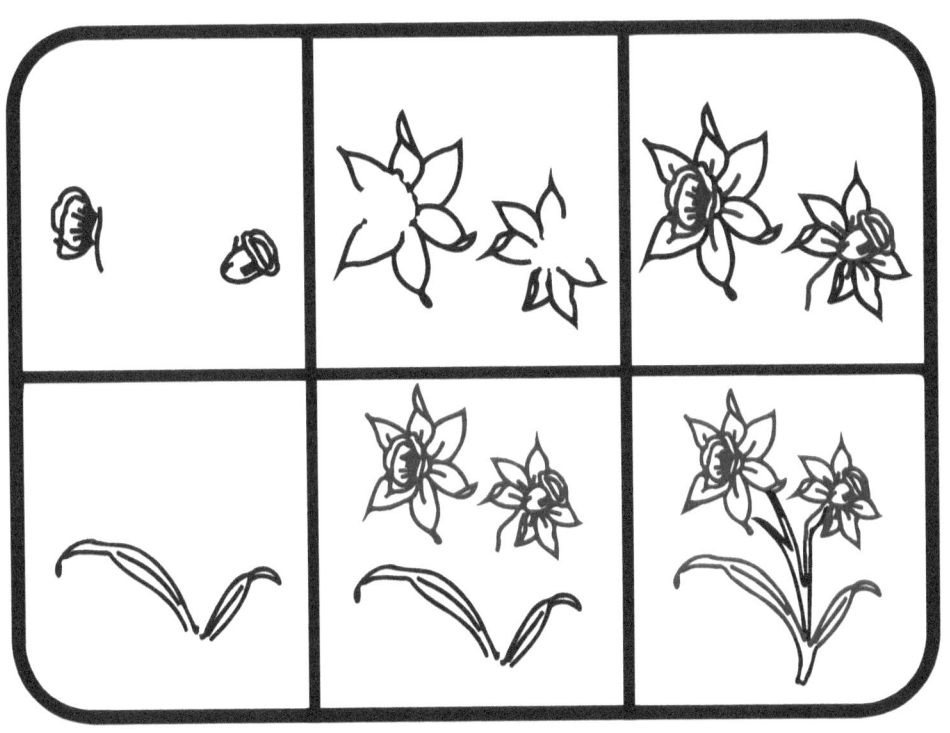

O Orange-Blossom

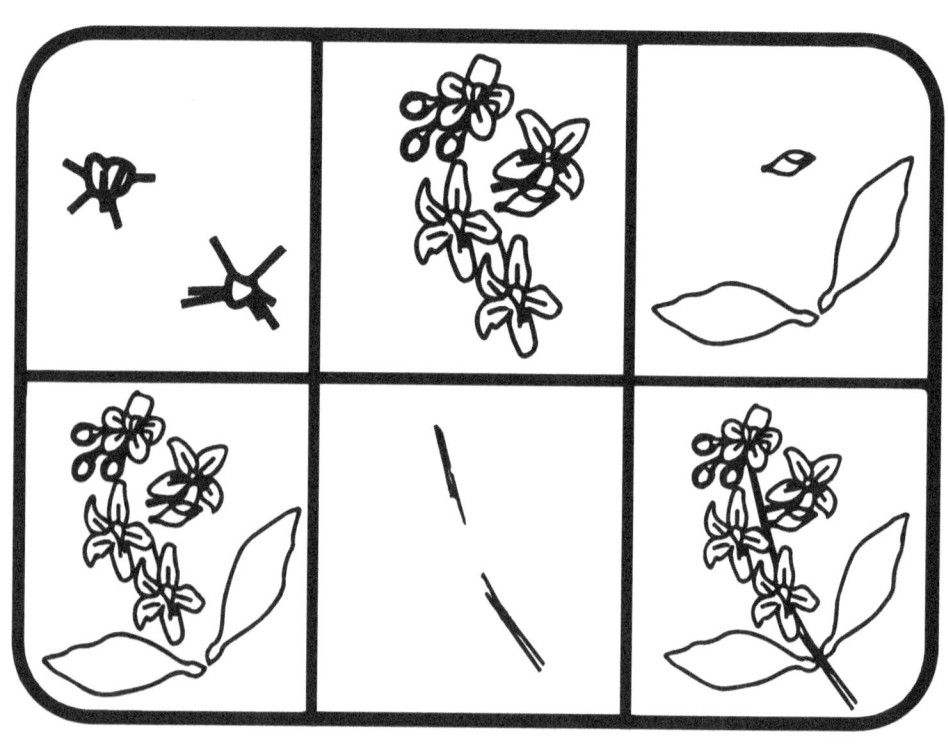

O

Ocho

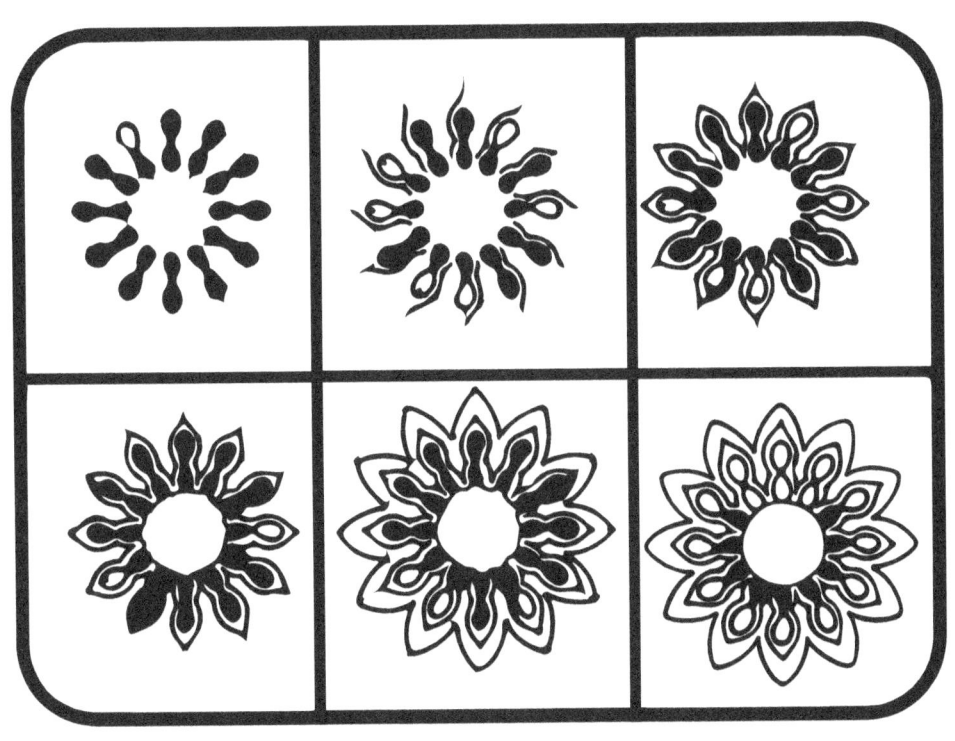

O Omni

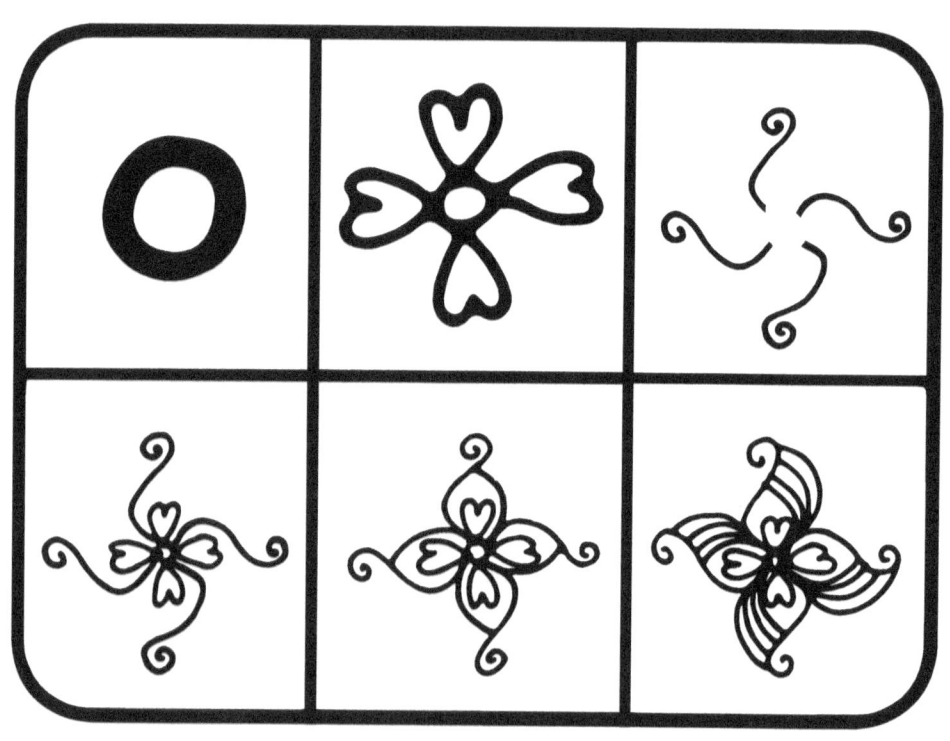

O Opia

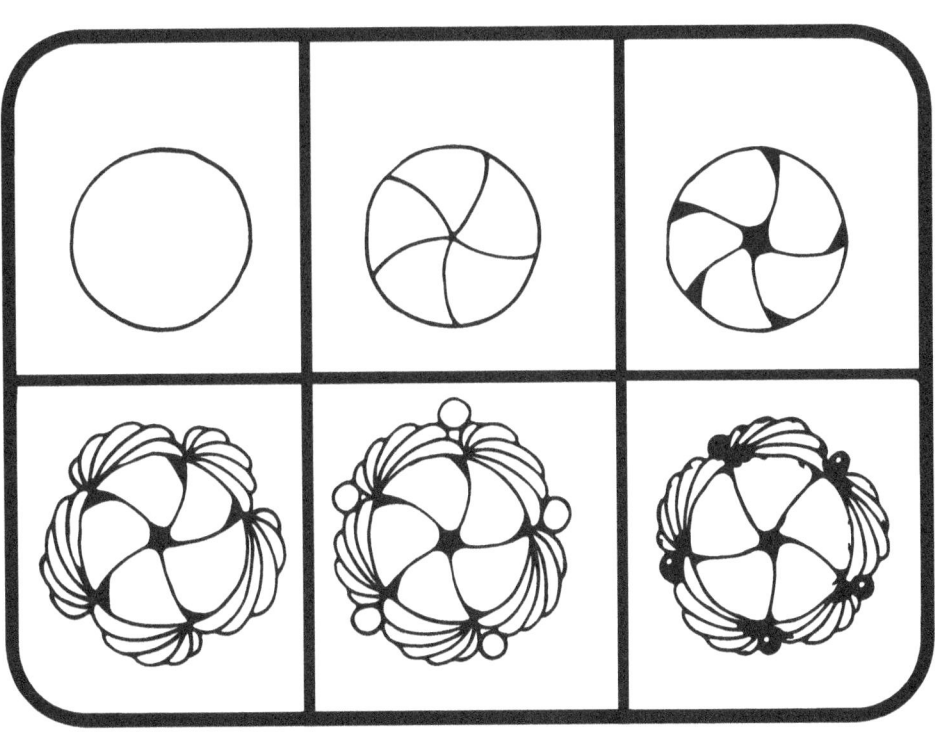

P

PussyWillow

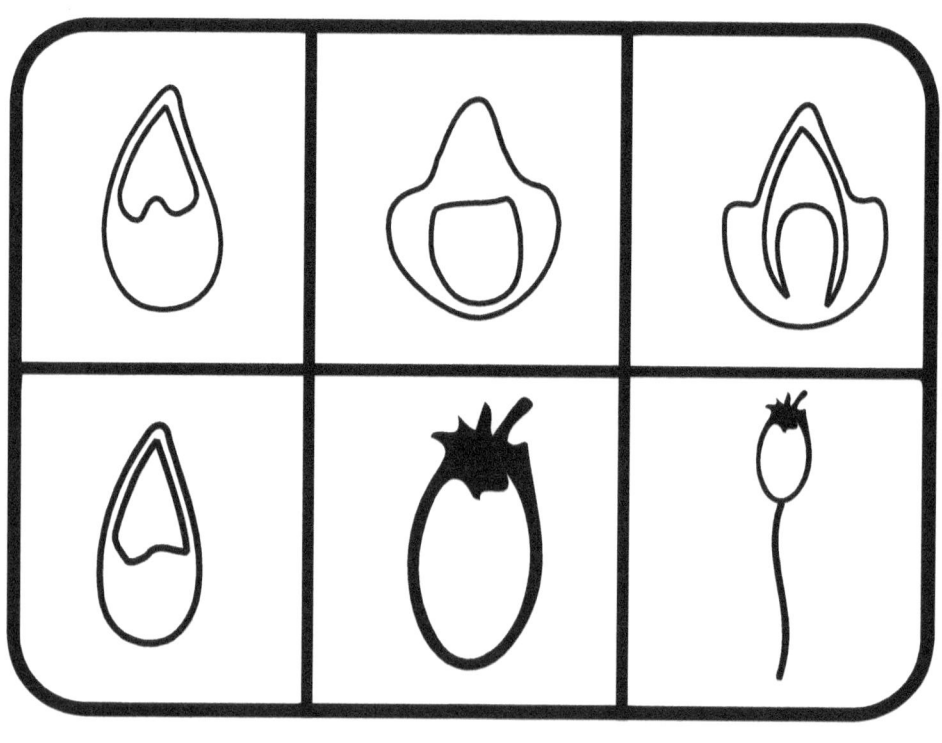

P Pansy

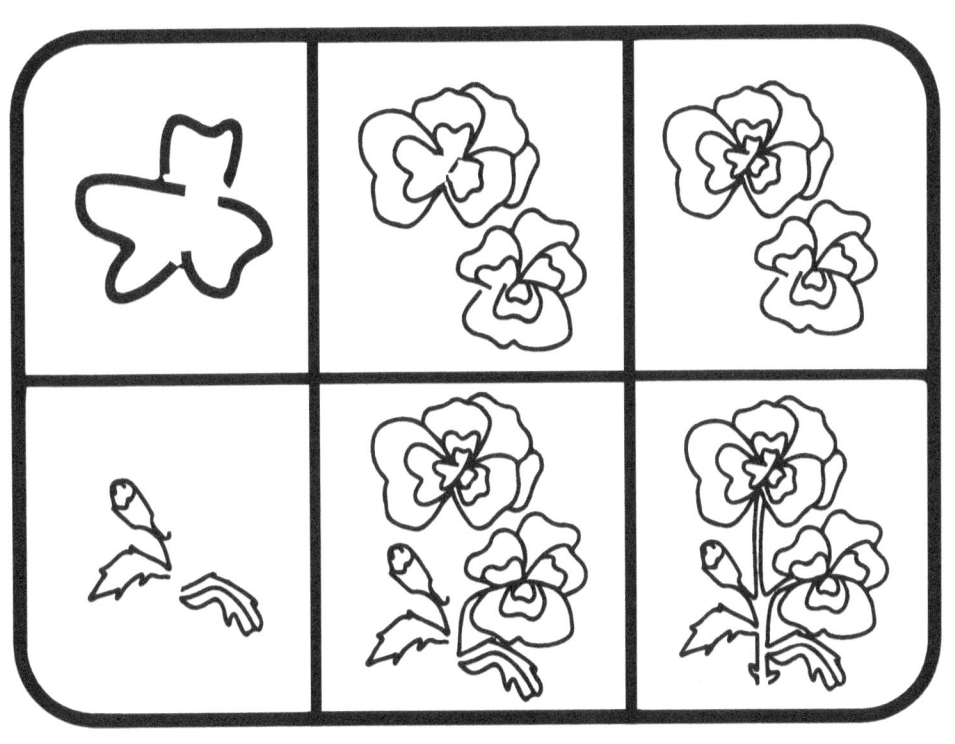

P
Peony

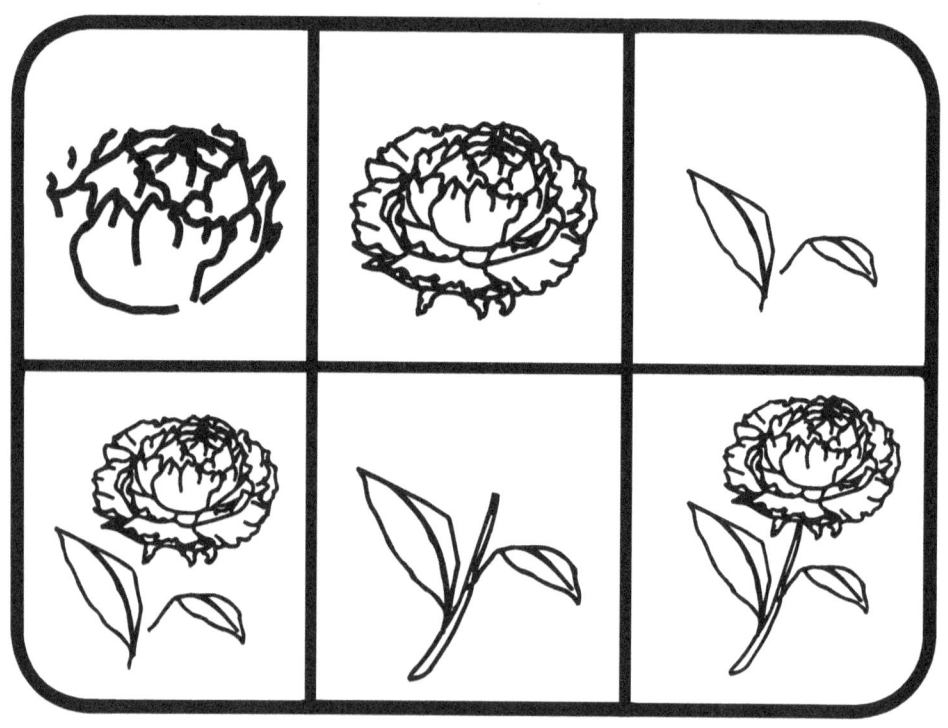

P

Periwinkle

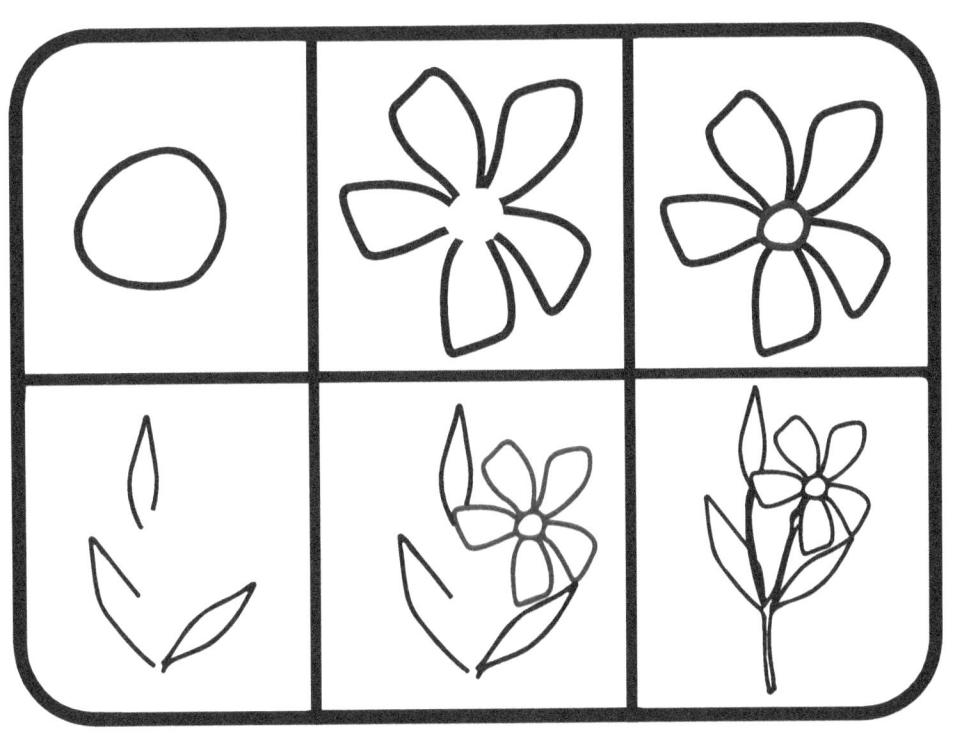

P

Pink

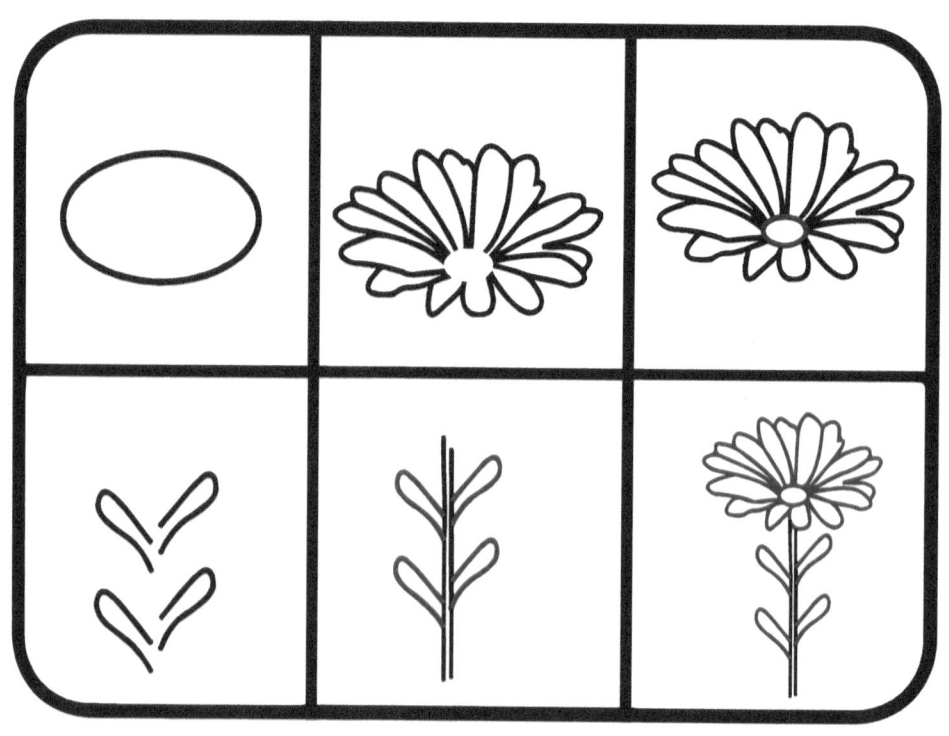

P
Poppy

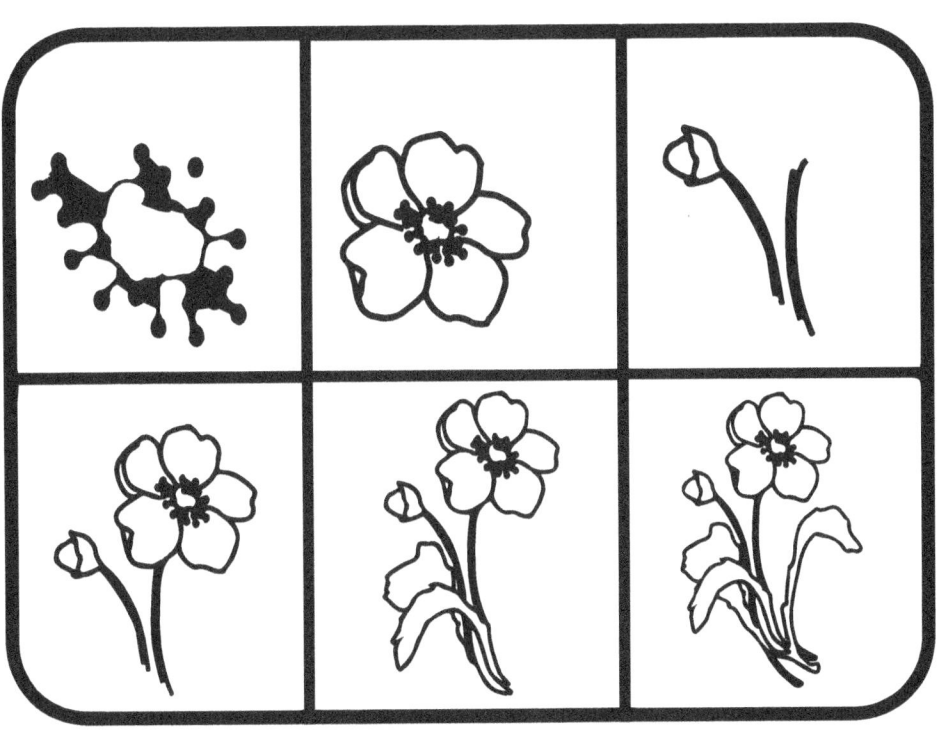

P
Primrose

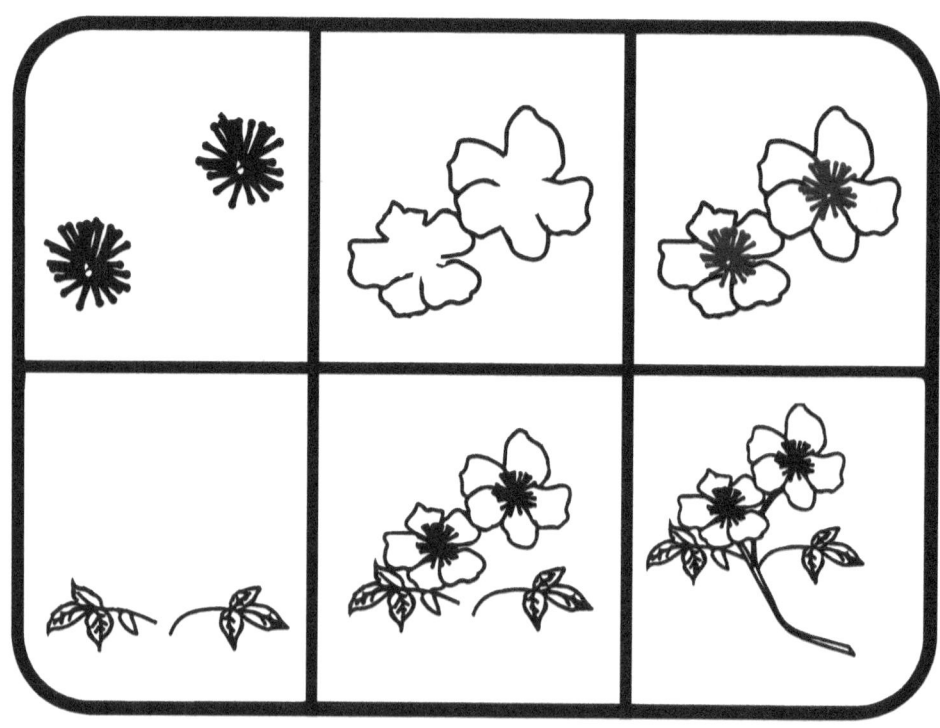

P Pax

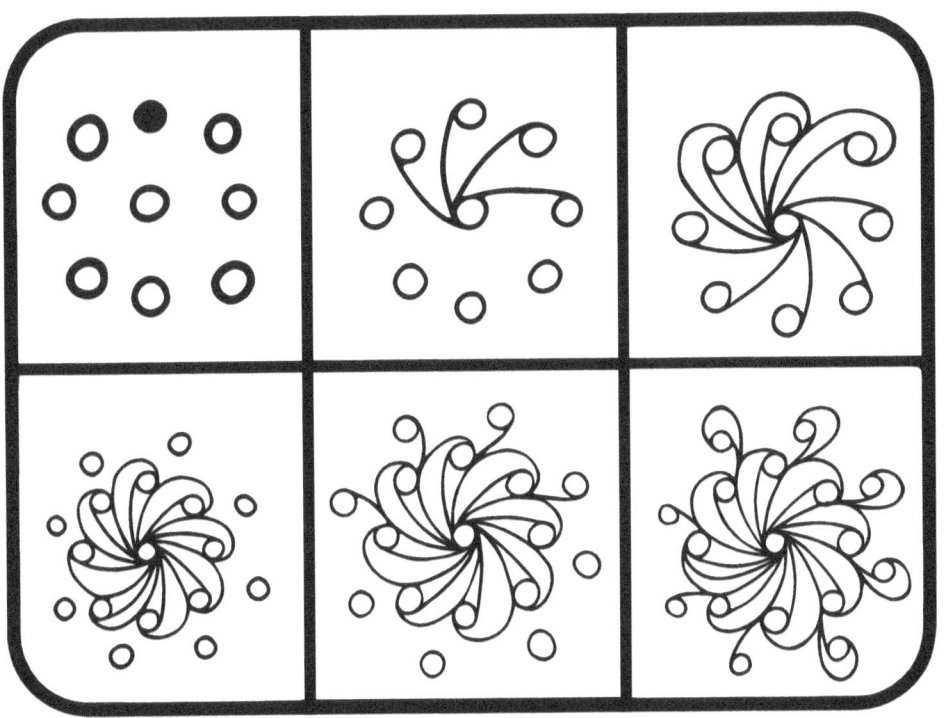

P

Pearlpod

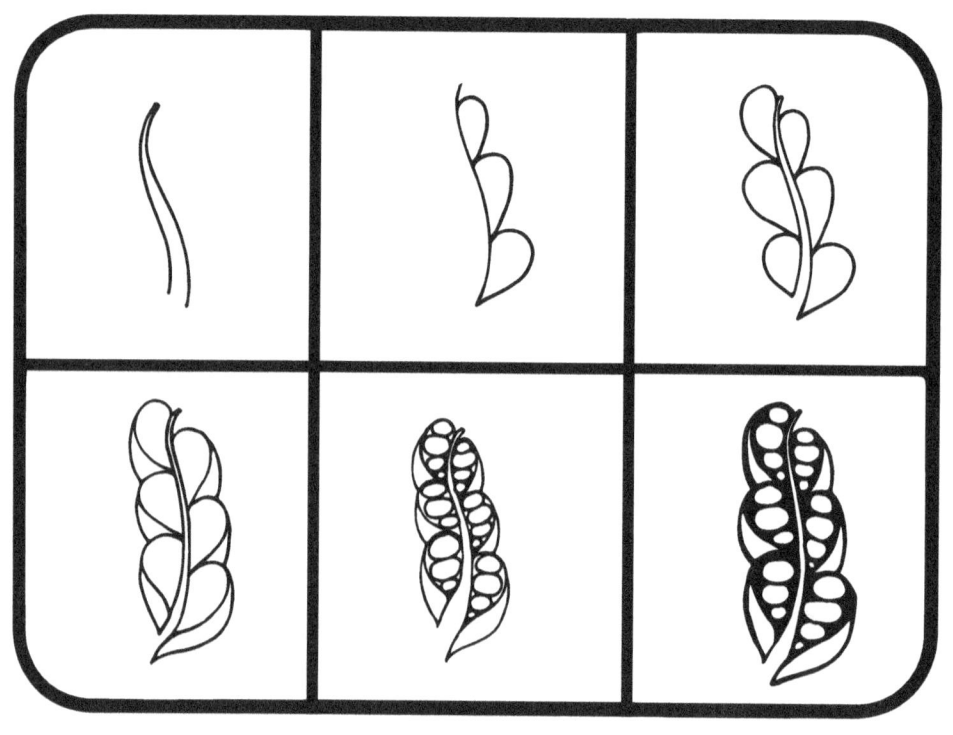

P

Panzee

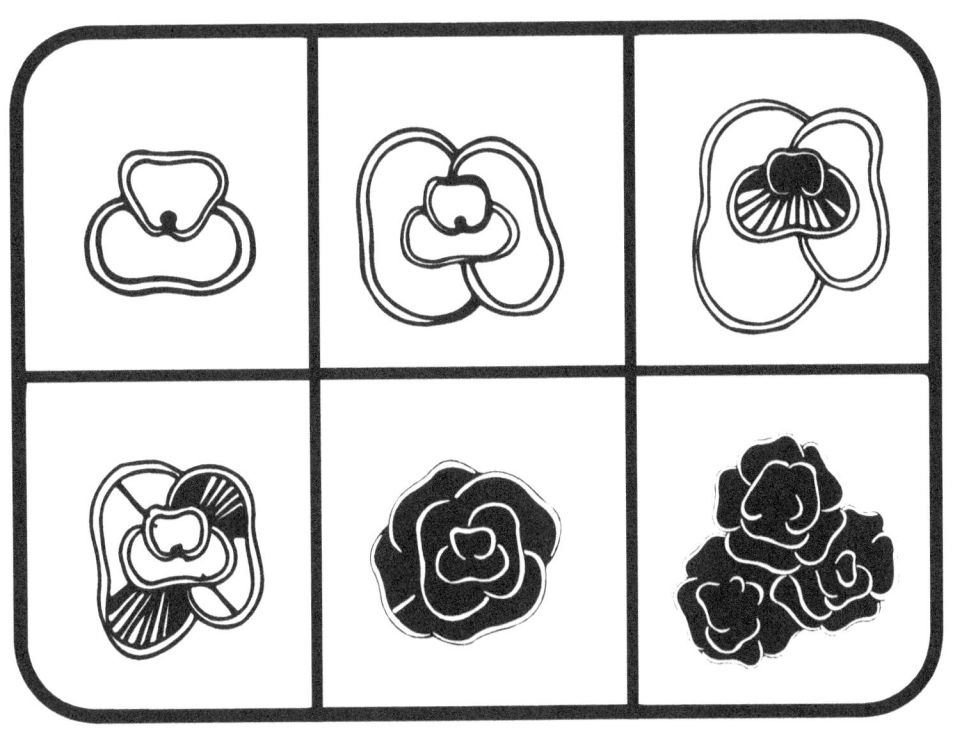

P

Putu Flower

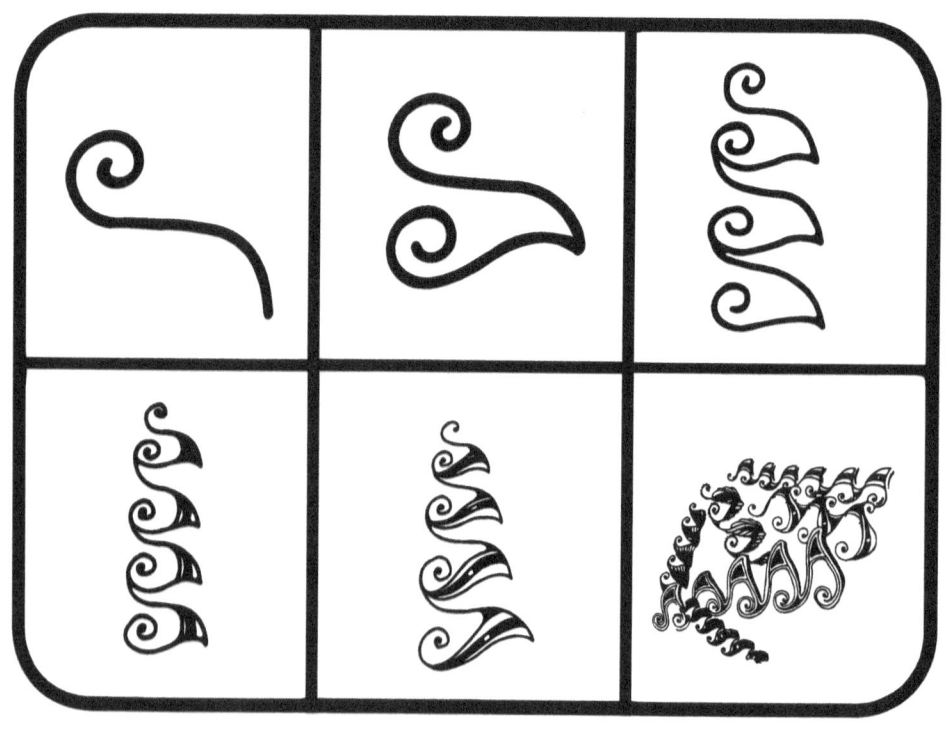

Q Quesnelia

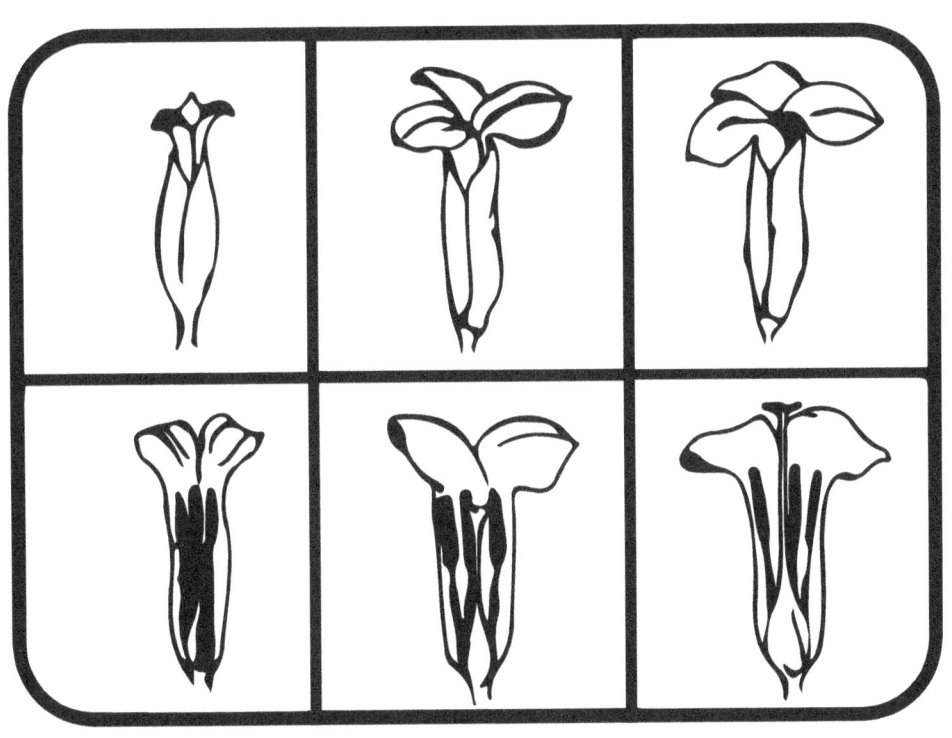

Q Queasy

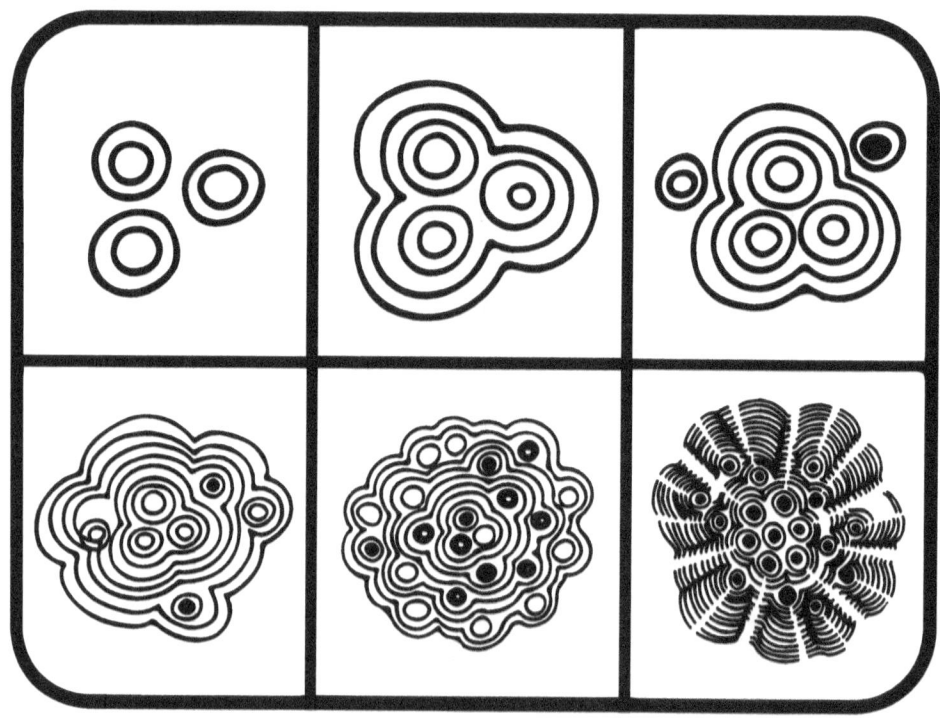

R Rose

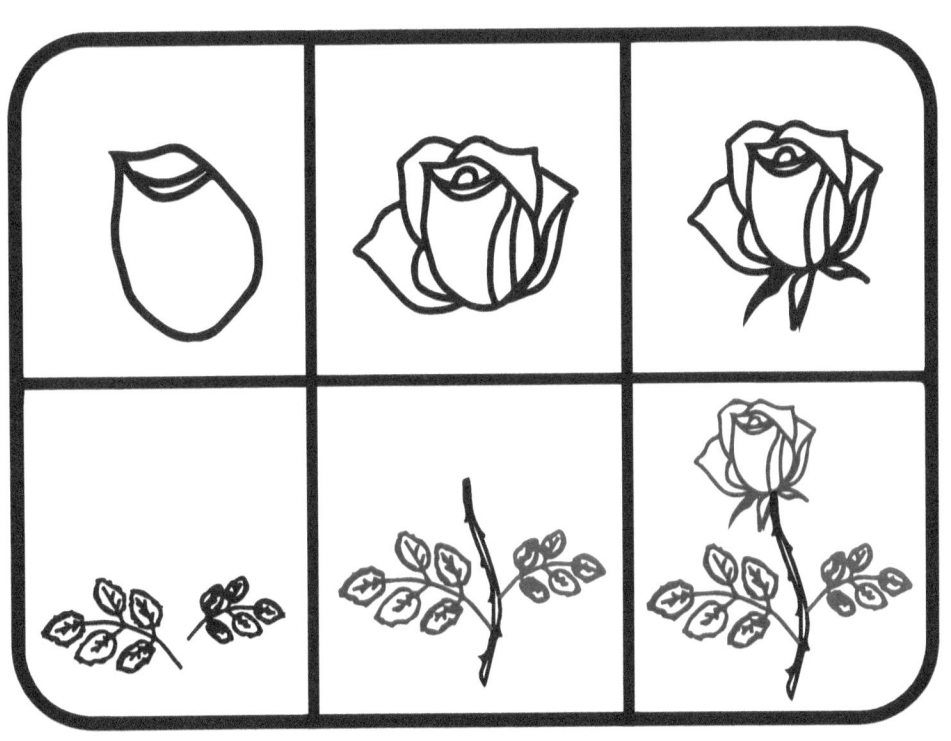

S Snowdrop

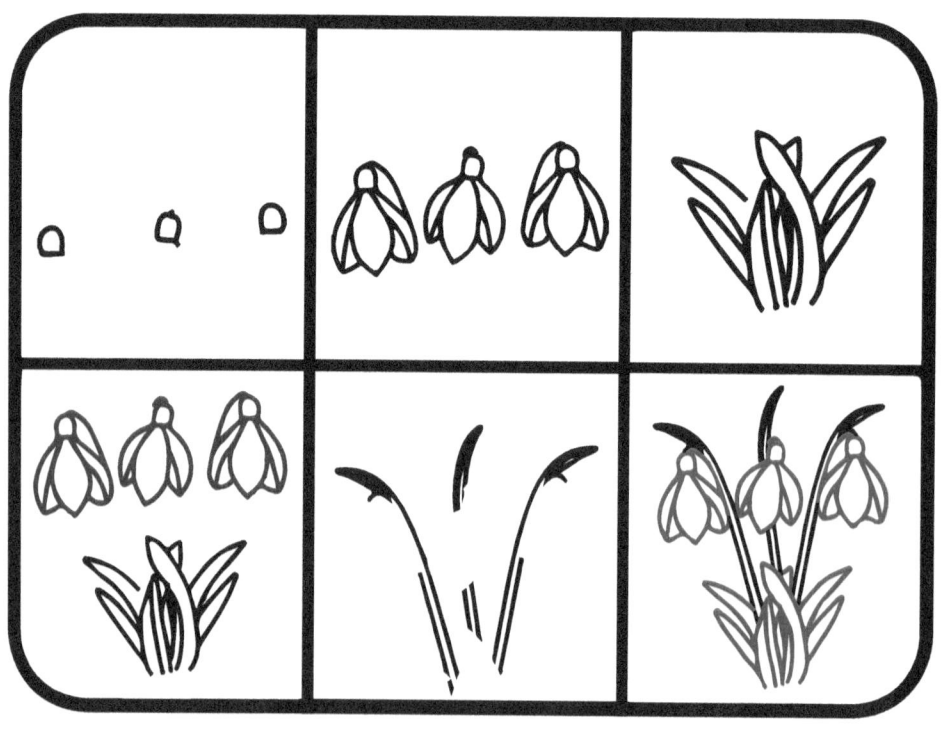

T Thistle

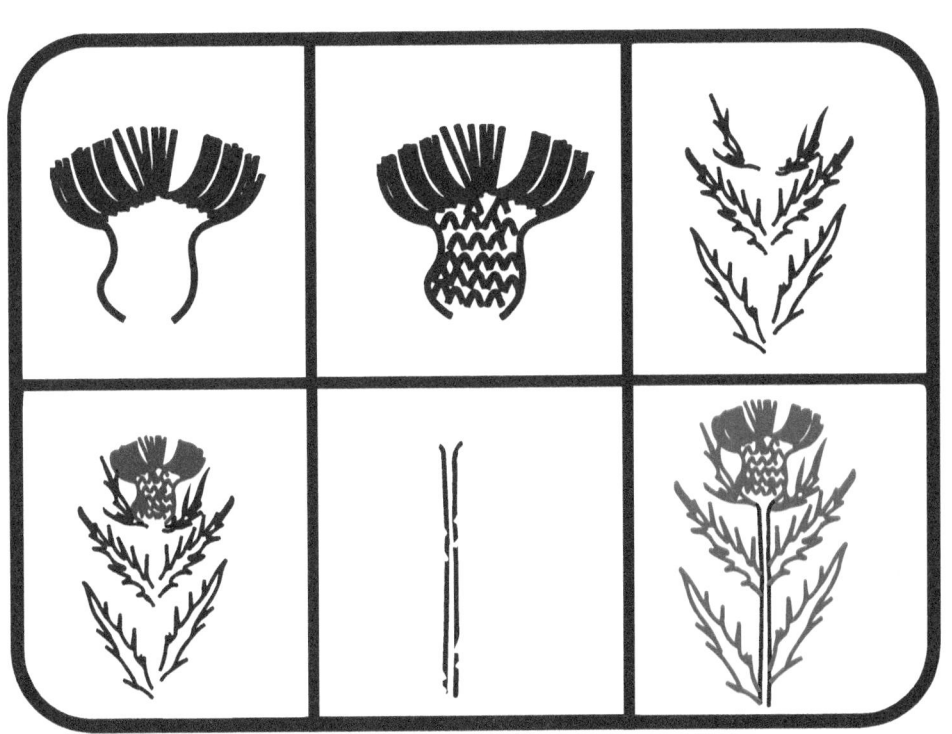

T Tulip

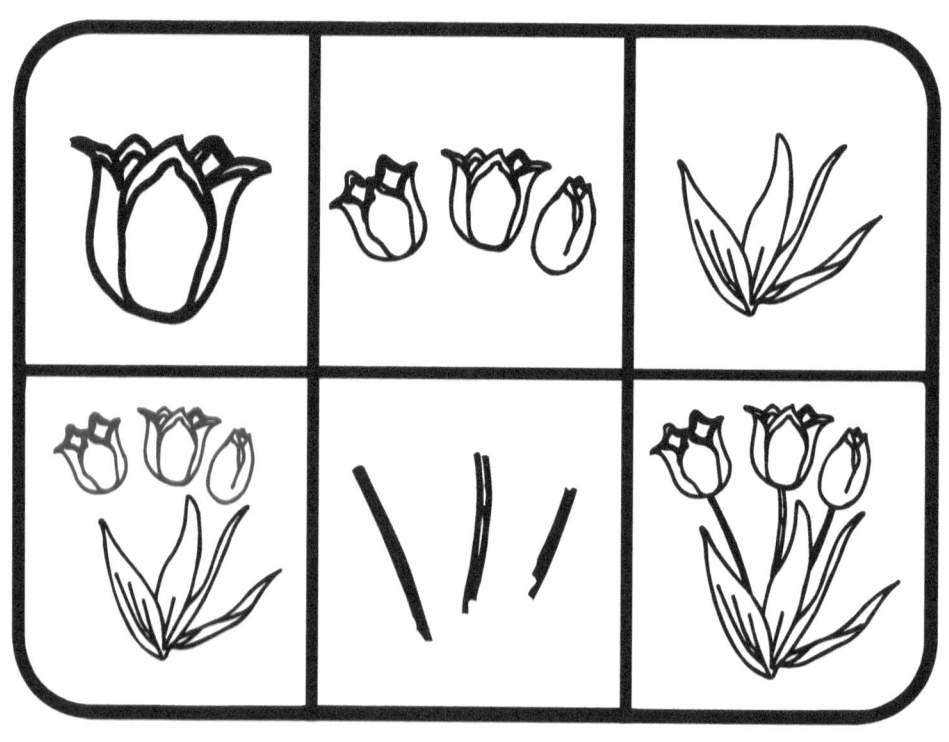

U
Ursinia

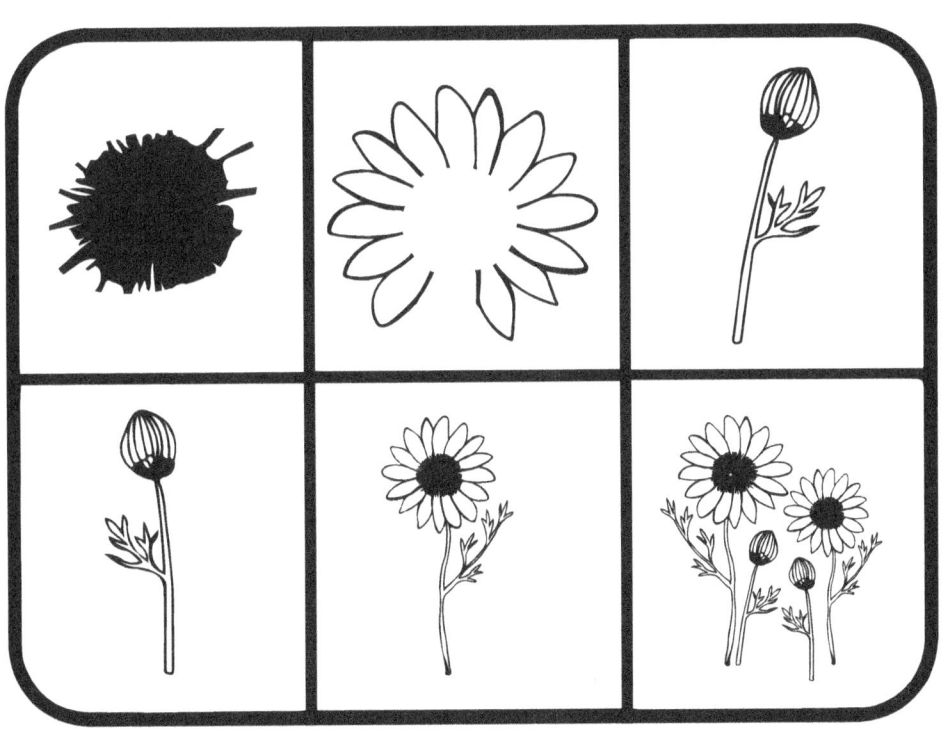

V Violet

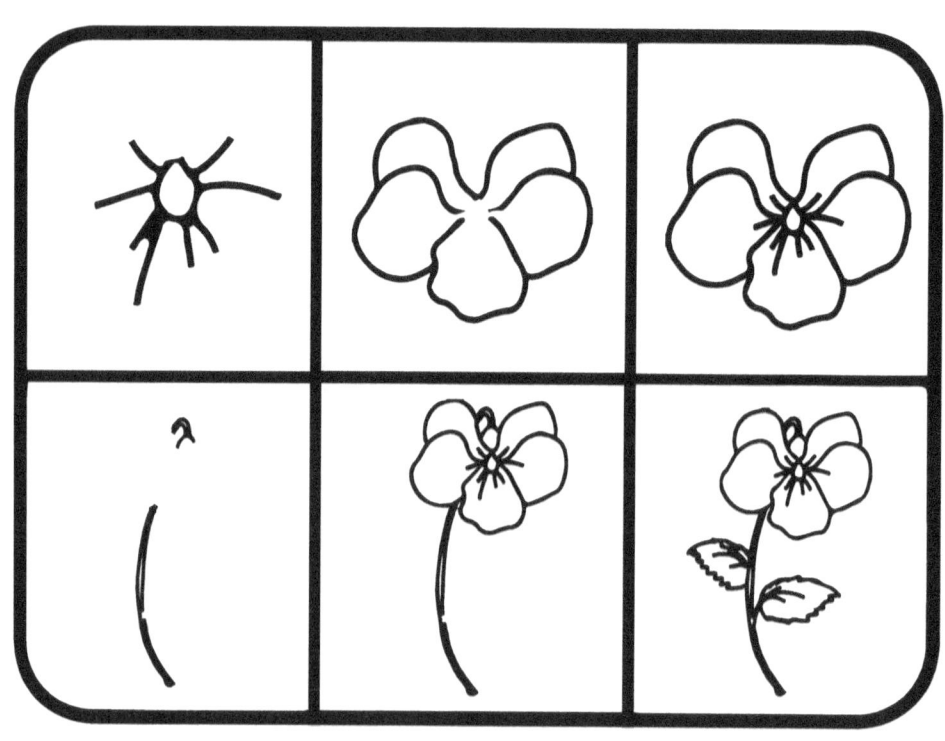

W Water-Lily

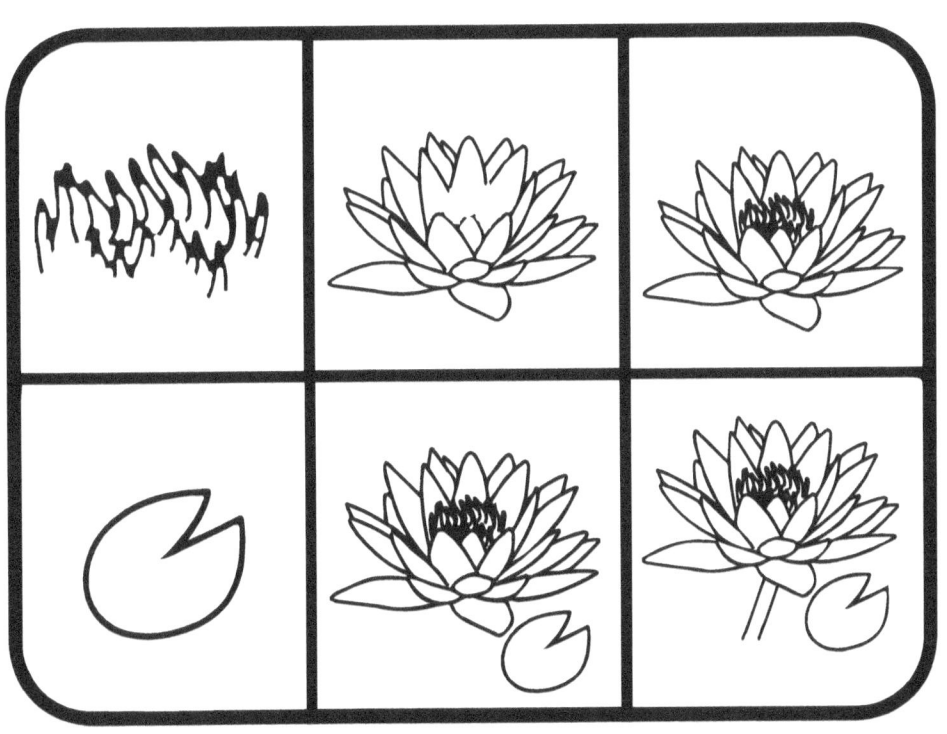

X Xeranthemum

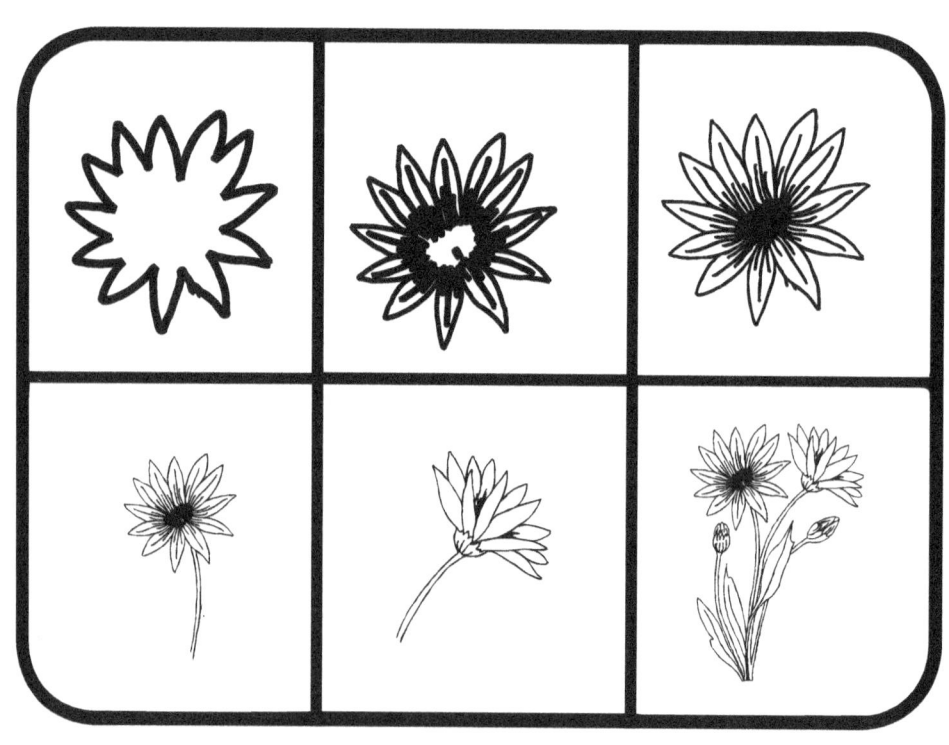

Y Yew

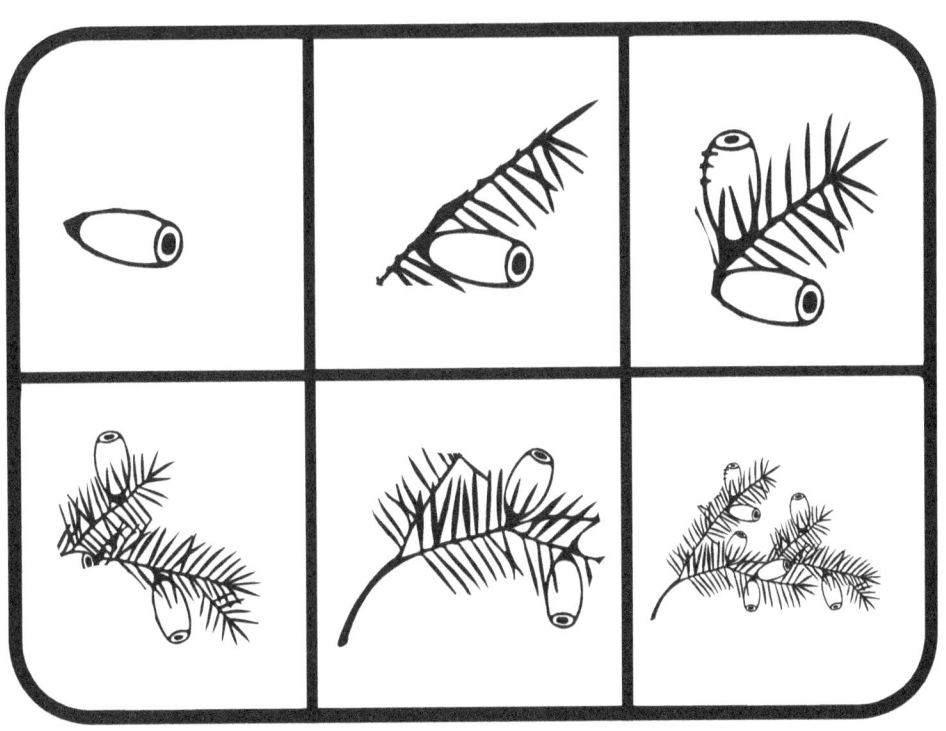

Z Zephyranthes

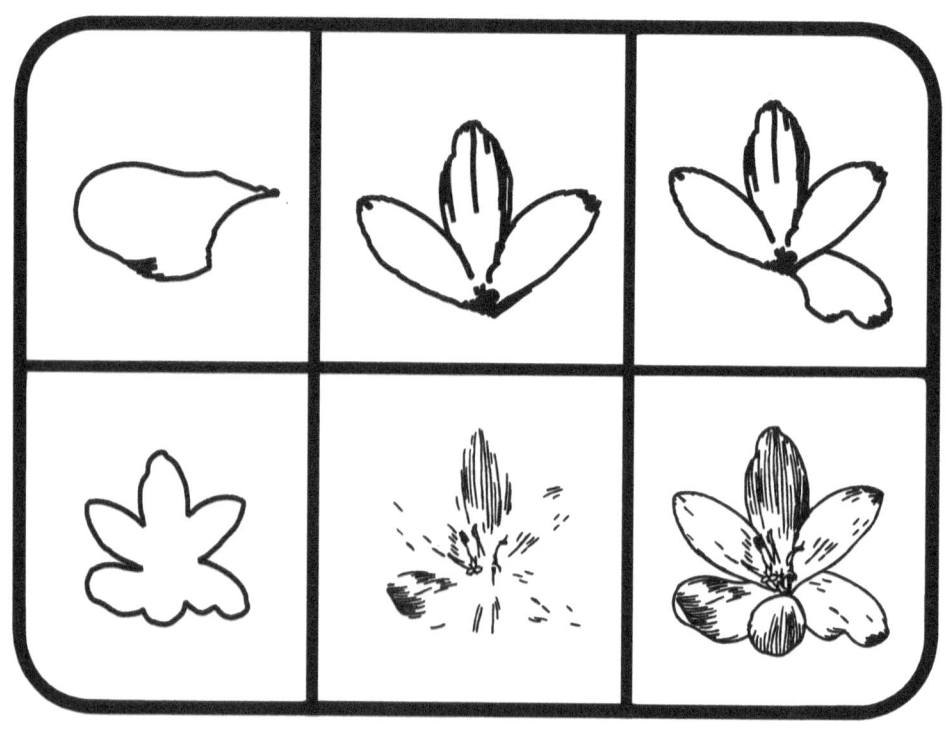